10 MINUTE GUIDE TO

NEGOTIATING

by Neil Shister

alpha books

Macmillan Spectrum/Alpha Books

A Division of Macmi

A Simon and Schuste

1633 Broadway, New

D1367439

International Standard Book Number: 0-02-861615-4
Library of Congress Catalog Card Number: 97-078167

99   8 7 6 5 4 3 2

Interpretation of the printing code: the rightmost double-digit number is the year of the book's first printing; the rightmost single-digit number is the number of the book's printing. For example, a printing code of 97-1 shows that this copy of the book was printed during the first printing of the book in 1997.

Printed in the United States of America

Note: Reasonable care has been taken in the preparation of the text to ensure its clarity and accuracy. This book is sold with the understanding that the author and the publisher are not engaged in rendering legal, accounting, or other professional service. Laws vary from state to state, and readers with specific financial questions should seek the services of a professional advisor.

The author and publisher specifically disclaim any liability, loss or risk, personal or otherwise, which is incurred as a consequence, directly or indirectly, of the use and application of any of the contents of this book.

Editor in Chief: Richard J. Staron

Production Editor: Michael Thomas

Copy Editor: Erik Dafforn

Cover Designer: Dan Armstrong

Designer: Glenn Larsen

Indexer: Jennifer Eberhardt

Production Team: Angela Calvert, Maureen West

Contents

INTRODUCTION

Neither education nor career prepared me to write a book about negotiation. At college I studied the humanities, by profession I was originally a journalist. What I know about negotiation I learned first by observing experts and then through practice. The information in this book is brief in format but dense in detail. It represents a distillation of several decades of practical instruction in the presence of masters. By being tactically armed in advance with the approach presented here, the reader hopefully will benefit from my experience without having to endure the painful process of being "out-negotiated" as often as I was.

Successful people, almost by definition, are successful negotiators. This is nearly always the case, although often how they go about getting what they want is so subtle it isn't readily apparent. The less obvious the negotiation, the more effective the negotiator! This realization originally got me interested in the process. Why were some people better than others at striking favorable deals? Two years in the Ivory Coast as a Peace Corps Volunteer provided first-hand practice in "marketplace bargaining," the banter of give-and-take used by buyer and seller in west Africa to establish price. As a reporter I got to observe assorted political negotiations, a rarefied form of discourse waged through the thinly veiled language of power. Later, by then an editor and subsequently publisher of publications, I became an actor in the decision-making process myself with a seat at the bargaining table.

In assorted roles I've worked with many skilled negotiators, each distinguished by their own way of doing things. Some are fastidiously polite, some blunt and to the point. Some seem to have been born negotiators, others have had to learn to be comfortable in the tug-and-pull of a conflict resolution. There are as many methods as there are negotiators. In this book, I've presented a fundamental approach which transcends style. Instead of recommending how to act, in this book I mostly suggest what to do: gather information, define objectives, listen attentively, speak carefully, stay focused on your ultimate goal. Stick to these principles and regardless of your temperament, whether you're bold as a lion or meek as a mouse, you can become a formidable negotiator.

One last note: Refuse to be intimidated! Even when the odds are most unlikely, few situations in life are rigidly fixed. Voicing a demand can't insure success, but failure to make a request guarantees it won't be realized. The golden rule to keep in mind, the mantra upon which to silently meditate as you enter into negotiation, is "Ask and you shall receive."

Of the many to whom I am grateful, one deserves special thanks for support and expert advice far beyond the cause of duty. Catherine Therese Clarke, whose humane instincts and strong-minded determination make her a formidable force for good, inspired this book. The most important negotiation this author ever participated in was when she agreed to be his wife.

CONVENTIONS USED IN THIS BOOK

This book uses three types of icons to help you quickly find important information:

 Tip icons offer ideas that cut corners and avoid confusion.

Plain English icons define new terms.

Panic Button icons identify potential problem areas and how to solve or avoid them.

About the Author

Neil Shister is an experienced negotiator who acquired his experience through on-the-job training as the founder of his own communications company in Atlanta, as Senior Vice President with the global public relations firm Hill & Knowlton, and as Vice President/Marketing with *Inc. Magazine* Business Resources.

A journalist by profession, Neil was a correspondent with *Time Magazine*, television critic for the *Miami Herald*, and Editor/ Publisher of *Atlanta Magazine* prior to entering business.

Shister lives in Cambridge, Massachusetts with his wife Catherine Therese Clarke-Shister, a constitutional law professor and legal scholar currently based at Harvard Law School.

Dedication

To my father, Joseph Shister, a life-long teacher in negotiations as well as other subjects; and to my mother, Edna Louise Shister, who gave me an appetite for exploration.

WHAT IS NEGOTIATION?

In this lesson you learn what negotiation is and how you can improve your life by negotiating for what you want.

Whenever you need the cooperation of another person to do something, however small, you are involved in a negotiation.

Almost everything we do—from deciding with a friend where to go to lunch to buying a new car to interviewing for a job—involves negotiating. The media portray negotiations as complicated, dramatic affairs involving powerful politicians or mighty business leaders or high-priced lawyers. But most often negotiations involve ordinary folks who, if they felt less intimidated by the process, would find themselves considerably more empowered in their lives.

Negotiation is not a magic rite. Nor is it rocket science requiring a Ph.D. Rather, it is a fundamental human act, the process that enables the trading of goods and services, favors and obligations. Negotiation is the protocol of exchange.

If negotiation is going on all the time, most often it is practiced without conscious attention. Instead of encouraging us to pursue results we desire, our culture regards the act of bargaining itself as somehow unseemly. It depicts the process as one in which two people try to take advantage of each other.

To identify your objectives and seek to obtain them strategically is thought to be manipulative, underhanded, "lacking in class."

So rather than try to negotiate strategically, most of us leave our negotiations to chance. Or assume that the other side will "play fair" (and then express outrage if they don't). Or pay a lawyer or broker to negotiate for us. Which is a shame.

INVESTING A LITTLE, GETTING A LOT

There are few social skills more useful than the ability to negotiate. To deny this is to deny one of the most fundamental human activities. From the Stone Age to the 21st century, history has moved forward through exchanging, bartering, and buying and selling services and products. In a word, through negotiation.

Despite what you may have been led to believe, the skills are easily learned. The principles are simple. They will take you on a fascinating journey of self-discovery in which you'll learn much about the nature of yourself, social relationships, and the economic marketplace.

And the personal payoff will be considerable and immediate. I guarantee it! By knowing how to negotiate you will exercise more leverage over your own life than you thought possible.

Negotiation The process by which at least two people (or sides) seek to make something happen. To be successful, both sides must agree with the resolution. This is just the beginning, however. Both sides must also cooperate in the implementation of the "contract" they have accepted.

Why go through all the hassle, you may ask? Why risk being pushy, aggressive, and offensive? *What's in it for me?* The answer is simple. *More of whatever you want!* Name it—time, money, respect, love, even peace of mind. As you become more adept at negotiation, you'll find yourself better equipped to influence what happens to you. You will be able to determine how you use your time, how much value you get for your money, and how others treat you.

To derive the benefits you seek, you need to proceed with an open mind. You must also suspend your expectations. If I can guarantee one thing about any negotiation, it is that something will happen that you never expected. Whether this surprise turns out good or bad for you depends on how prepared you are for just this turn of events. As baseball player Yogi Berra might have said, "It ain't over until it's over."

 The Law of Unanticipated Results Never assume you know how events are going to play out, what the other side wants, or how they will react. Always expect the unexpected.

The appeal of negotiations is that they encourage flexibility. Both sides bend. To the supple go the rewards. Why? Because both parties come to see that their interests are best served by working together, even at the cost of giving up some of their own advantages.

The art of negotiation is presenting your point of view (and responding to the other side's) in a way that encourages this flexibility. That means knowing how the game is played.

Negotiation is a process that has no fixed rules but follows a predictable pattern. It is very much like a sporting event of two contesting wills, complete with advance game plans, strategic ploys, and bursts of brilliant open-field running.

Unlike most contests, though, a negotiation doesn't have to end up with a winner and loser. At the end there may not even be a score to tally. A well-conducted negotiation may allow both sides to win by expanding the total pot, making the sum for both sides greater than either could possess alone. In the language of academics this is called "synergy."

Here's a hypothetical example. You manufacture widgets. A customer with a one-year contract wants service faster than you can provide because you lack the staff and machinery. He threatens to take his business elsewhere. If you knew this customer would buy in volume over a long period, you could put on extra labor and add a machine. The two of you choose to negotiate. In return for speedier delivery, the customer signs a five-year contract. Win-win.

Or take an example closer to home. Whenever you ask your teenager to help around the house, she mounts a firefight worthy of Operation Desert Storm. At the same time, she complains that she can't drive the family car to the mall whenever she wants. Instead of screeching and screaming every night, you both agree to negotiate a solution. Perhaps each time she does a chore without complaint, she earns one hour's use of the car with no questions asked (or something to that effect; the specific rules are up to your negotiation). The chores get done, and she doesn't have to beg for the car. You both win and, in the process, create something that is bigger than the resolution of the specific issues. You have created a stable communication process instead of ongoing shouting matches, a "structure of exchange" (clean room in return for car privileges), and, ideally, more domestic tranquility.

The better negotiator you become, the more likely you are to leave situations better off than you found them. Scorched earth is for amateurs! By analyzing yourself and your intentions, perfecting your ability to listen better, and learning how to structure a solution suitable for mutual benefit, you can become a master negotiator.

But there's another side to the coin. A little knowledge can sometimes be a dangerous thing. Instead of encouraging accommodation, a negotiation can sometimes dissolve into a brutal battle of egos. Positions become as fixed as the trenches of World War I—and the results are nearly as bloody—when both sides refuse to give in.

Issues involving personality and critical comments about the other side's honesty, truthfulness, and reliability can undermine an orderly process. The same thing happens when you bring up ill will from the past—when you try to use a current negotiation to get revenge for a previous insult. It's never helpful to use today's negotiation to seek payback for yesterday's grievance. Be on your guard against this, for when it happens, the hole of retribution is being dug deeper.

Look at the same hypothetical situation from a different perspective. Your widget customer wants better service. You think he's trying to hold you up again, since he paid late last year and left you in a tough bind. You figure his request is just a smokescreen; you're sure what he really wants is to break the contract. Instead of negotiating in good faith, you stonewall—"Like it or leave it." The customer, angry at you for being stubborn, goes to your competitor at the end of the year. You're left holding the bag and end up losing business.

The shrewd Mark H. McCormack, whose company bargains in behalf of star athletes, says that in the final analysis it is personal qualities that distinguish a great negotiator. To be a good negotiator you must have certain traits: knowing what makes people tick, enjoying a competitive tussle, being able to see the big picture without losing sight of critical details. But in the end, says McCormack, it is unimpeachable integrity that most counts. In his book *On Negotiating* (Dove Books, 1995), he says that "If I'm convinced of the other side's sense of honor and fair play, I'll usually let them get away with negotiating points that I would fight over with more slippery people."

Don't Get Personal   Steer clear of personal antagonism in your negotiations. Be alert to personal agendas, both yours and the other side's. Resist the temptation to bring up the past as you deal with the present. If the other side does so, suggest that it reduces the likelihood of a win-win solution (squabbling over "who did what to whom way back when" is an endless argument that never gets resolved).

REMEMBER THE GOLDEN RULE: ASK AND YE SHALL RECEIVE

This isn't to say that you shouldn't be assertive. Just the opposite. The starting point on the road to becoming a master negotiator is with The Golden Rule of Negotiation, the first action principle: *Tell the other side what you want or you'll probably never get it.* This is the "fulcrum" that allows you to leverage the returns you'll receive from your time, energy, and money. This simple principle should be so obvious it is self-evident, but you'd be surprised how difficult it is for some people to express their needs and desires.

Never Be Afraid to Ask Let the other side say "no" for themselves. But when you ask for something, be prepared to give up something in return.

The essence of negotiation is to make your request loud and clear so the other side hears it. Yet many of us are afraid to do just that. We're too embarrassed to make a demand. We fear rejection. We don't want to make the other side angry. We are immobilized by our own timidity. What we are doing, in effect, is having an internal conversation with ourselves that goes like this: "They'll never agree to let me have what I want, so there's no point in even asking." What you've done in such an internal dialogue is *ensure failure!* You've set yourself up to say "no" for the other side.

If you fail to make the request without having given up a thing, the other side is already ahead! You've made things easy for them! How? For starters, you've eliminated the possibility that they might actually say yes. Or that perhaps, after hearing your request, they might agree to a compromise solution that is equally desirable.

One of my early negotiating assignments was as a broker in the sale of a home security business to a large British conglomerate eager to enter the American market. My client was a highly successful international real estate developer who had executed dozens of multimillion-dollar deals. Although I was the go-between, he was really the master negotiator. As the bargaining grew heated, I relayed the latest offers. "Tell them we want twice as much," he said. "They'll never go for that," I answered. "Just do it," he insisted, impatient with my timidity. Sure enough, they bought it. What did they want in return?

To stretch the payout over twice as much time. Again, I thought this unreasonable. Sure enough, my client agreed. Just goes to show the unexpected in action!

I learned the lesson. Make the other side say no for themselves! Even if you think they'll never accept your offer, put it out there anyway. Give them the opportunity to make up their own mind! You'll be positively amazed how often they exercise their legitimate option to say yes. *A negotiation is a dialogue of possibilities; you are responsible for saying what you want.*

tip   **Simple as Pie**   There's no mystery to negotiating. All you have to know is how!

In this lesson you learned what negotiation is and how you can improve your life by negotiating for what you want.

THE GREAT DIVIDE: "TAKE NO PRISONERS" VS. "LET'S MAKE A DEAL"

In this lesson you learn the importance of a win-win approach and how to create the right attitude.

Negotiations are required when there is a problem to work out, such as a transaction to make, a crisis to resolve, or assets to divide. The act of acknowledging mutual interests and coming together is an important first step, but getting to the table neither ensures the nature of the process nor guarantees the results.

The mood in which the sides arrive at the negotiation greatly influences the outcome. They can arrive angry, vindictive, and filled with animosity. Intent on getting every last crumb of value left on the table. Not content until the other side grovels powerless in the dust. (An example of this scenario is a bitter divorce settlement in which a long-suffering spouse, cast aside for a rival, is intent on vengeance.) Or they can arrive open-minded, reasonable, and prepared to compromise.

At its worst, negotiation is sublimated violence. At its best, it's a civilized process calculated to maximize accord. What decides which way the balance tilts? Essentially it's a matter of intention: whether the two sides choose to work *with* each other or *against* each other. That decision, how to approach the other side, is the most critical choice in a negotiation.

The shootout model constitutes one approach. In this mode, each disputant takes on a self-righteous air, facing his opponent with the single-minded determination of a gunslinger in a showdown in which only one person is going to leave alive. In such a negotiation, each side is so wholly invested in its point of view that compromise is unthinkable.

A visceral thrill exists in this kind of negotiation; playing the "tough guy" (or gal) has a romantic appeal reinforced by abundant cultural messages (Hollywood is particularly fond of such confrontations). This is also the model for litigation ("So sue me!"). In *The Tao of Negotiation* (Harper Business, 1994), Joel Edelman and Mary Beth Crain note that "conflict is a kind of drug," which explains why this impulse can be so hard to resist. "Aggressive behavior provides us with a 'high' ... it's exhilarating for many people to 'beat' someone else." The intoxication of competition, of annihilating your opponent, can be addictive.

I call the other kind of negotiation "let's make a deal." The parties come together not to annihilate each other, but to find a solution. They are aware that they maximize their respective benefits by recognizing their mutual dependency. This is the "win-win" model. The bad news is that it requires more discipline and self-awareness, more patience and vision. The good news is that it's more likely to produce lasting success. When the ideal is to "expand the pie," we're talking about "let's make a deal."

Win-Win Situation   When both parties satisfy their key objectives and are sufficiently pleased with the process to negotiate again. The overarching factor that creates a win-win situation is an ongoing dialogue of mutual give-and-take, not take-it-or-leave-it macho bluster.

DETERMINING THE STRUCTURE OF CONFLICT

It is one thing to encourage a win-win situation and quite another to actually implement it. The reason? Regardless of one's intentions, every negotiation contains real disagreements that can't simply be dismissed or papered over. In order to move through these without getting frozen in an impasse, it is important to be able to adjust the process to different kinds of conflict.

- **One-sided vs. two-sided conflict:** In a unilateral conflict, only one side has a request and is petitioning the other side for permission or approval (for example, an employee asks the boss for permission to leave early for personal reasons even though it is inconvenient). In a bilateral conflict, each side has an objective to accomplish and no resolution can exist until both are satisfied.

- **Personal grievances vs. "The System":** Some conflicts result from acts of individual volition, whereas some are the result of rules and procedures that transcend the people involved. John and Mary are neighbors; he has a noisy dog and she has a loud stereo. They have a history of conflict that flares into a nasty dispute. This is *personal*.

Peter is the shop manager whose objective is to maximize output, and Sally is the union representative whose objective is to safeguard the workers. They have a history of conflict that flares into a nasty dispute. This is *systemic* because their disagreements are the result of the different organizational agendas that they represent.

Don't Get Personal   System disputes are not personal (even though there can often be personality frictions involved). Do not confuse positions that are determined by external factors or social conditioning with the people who voice them. Separate the issues from the actors.

IDENTIFYING PERSONAL ISSUES THAT THREATEN WIN-WIN SITUATIONS

The foundation of a win-win negotiation is mutual respect. Both sides need to believe that the other side is sincere in its intention to seek mutually acceptable compromise. After good faith breaks down, it is very hard to repair.

Good faith breaks down for several reasons:

- **Innocent misunderstanding.** Precaution: Clarify the reasons for your actions and positions; never take it for granted that the other side knows what you believe or why you're doing something.

- **Perceived dishonesty.** Precaution: Mean what you say and say what you mean. If you've erred, say so right away. Cover-ups clog the channels of communication like cholesterol in the arteries. Half-truths, unspoken truths, and deceptions can be just as destructive as outright lies. Have the courage to be honest.

- **Negligence and irresponsibility.** Precaution: If you say you'll do something, do it! Be on time. Respect confidences. Honor commitments. Treat the other side with the same respect you expect. Don't overstep boundaries.

- **Fear.** Precaution: Ease any irrational fears the other side may have. Negotiations unleash feelings of threat and exposure, so make the other side feel safe. Assure them that your position does not constitute a repudiation of their deeply held beliefs or sense of self.

Treasure Your Reputation   The other side's belief in your good faith is your most valuable asset. Nurture it like a treasure! If your honesty becomes questionable, you will always have to prove you're not a liar. Concessions will not erase the lasting impact of the loss of good faith.

Unleashing the Power of One

The mood of a negotiation, whether shootout or win-win, can be influenced by how you approach the process, regardless of the other side! If you project a reasoned, objective, enlightened attitude, it acts as an antidote to the pollutants of unbridled conflict. By being sensitive to the forces that undermine good faith, you can resist being dragged under by them. If you refuse to fight but steadfastly adhere to the win-win philosophy, you will neutralize most imbalances. In other words, stick to the high ground.

 You Hold the Key   It takes one to resolve dispute by seeking a solution. It takes two to prolong conflict.

WORKSHEET: AM I WIN-WIN ORIENTED?

	Always	Sometimes	Never
People usually understand what I mean	___	___	___
I am on time	___	___	___
If I say I'll do something, I do it	___	___	___
I take offense quickly	___	___	___
I usually know what's best	___	___	___
People find me off-putting when I don't mean to be	___	___	___
I explain situations fully	___	___	___
I don't disclose all information	___	___	___
I admit mistakes	___	___	___

	Always	Sometimes	Never
Different lifestyles upset/ offend me	___	___	___
I am usually right	___	___	___

Recall a significant argument or dispute that you have been involved in (the more recent, the better):

What was the dispute about?

Was the dispute one-sided or two-sided?

Was the dispute personal or systemic?

Were the negotiations friendly or fierce?

Was the communication process open or strained?

How was the dispute resolved?

Could you and the other side negotiate in the future or does bad will remain?

In this lesson you learned the importance of a win-win approach and how to create the right attitude.

3

HOW TO RECOGNIZE A NEGOTIATION SITUATION

In this lesson you learn how to recognize an opportune negotiating situation.

By virtue of being social beings, humans exist amidst endless networks of mutual interest. Sometimes these relationships work smoothly, sometimes they are fraught with friction and conflict. Either way, however, nearly everything you do involves another person.

UNDERSTANDING THE UNIVERSALITY OF MUTUAL INTERESTS

Consider an average day. Think of how your daily actions intersect with the goals and objectives of others. At home, the members of your family rely on each other for grand things such as love and sustenance and for considerably lesser acts such as being driven to soccer practice, preparing dinner, and paying the electricity bill. In the marketplace, there can't be a buyer without a seller. If you work in a company, you're probably part of a team created to implement shared goals and objectives. Even if you work alone you depend on the mail carrier.

At each center of mutual interest there is a transaction of one thing for another, such as goods for money, time for service, or labor for compensation. The trade can be on a grand scale, such as exchanging millions of dollars for real estate assets. Or it can be strictly personal, such as a woman deciding whether to accept an invitation to go on a date.

Big or small, negotiation opportunities abound—everywhere, and all the time. In many situations you're accustomed to bargaining—buying an automobile or selling a house, for example. But many other negotiation situations might never occur to you:

- Shopping for clothes
- When relatives pay a visit
- Your boss makes an excessive demand
- The bank errs
- Your computer fails to function
- A flight is overbooked

The list is limitless. *These are all opportunities to negotiate.*

It's Everywhere!   Although most people don't realize it, you can negotiate for just about anything just about anywhere. Any interaction that entails an exchange can become a negotiation. The only thing that prohibits you from initiating a negotiation is not recognizing the situation.

tip   **Seize the Possibility**   We are almost always in negotiation. Sometimes we realize it, and sometimes we don't. The advantage always goes to the side that first realizes the availability of options.

DECIDING WHETHER TO PROCEED

Although negotiation opportunities abound, most of us don't spend large parts of our days bargaining. Rightfully so. There are other things to do with higher priorities! We could spend two hours bargaining with the manager of the food store over how much to pay for brussels sprouts or we could get on with our lives! Thus even if a potential negotiation situation exists, we do not always choose to invoke the process.

Deciding whether to negotiate depends on the answers to several questions:

DO THE STAKES JUSTIFY THE COMBAT?

Just as a warrior doesn't go into battle every time a slight nuisance is encountered, neither should a negotiator haul out the heavy artillery without good cause. Any negotiation entails some cost, time, effort, and good will.

Value is a matter of personal choice; some people contest pennies while others dismiss dollars. Everybody's scale of worth is different. The important thing is to evaluate the situation carefully according to your own standards in advance of entering into a negotiation.

Do Potential Gains Exceed the Risks of Loss?

If a negotiation might win you a penny but put a dollar at risk, is the process worthwhile? What about if you stand the chance of winning a battle but losing the war?

Risk/benefit analysis allows you to weigh the positives and negatives of a situation. If you decide the rewards are trivial compared to what you may have to give up, it's probably best to move on. Another opportunity will always come along.

How Much Flexibility Can You Expect from the Other Side?

Imagine a continuum with irreconcilable conflict at one end (Bosnia in the midst of genocidal civil war, for instance) and universal good will at the other (such as a celebratory gathering of a company's top sales performers at its annual retreat in the Bahamas). In the first example, positions are so fixed that neither side can accept the good faith of the other. In the second, there is such universality of agreement ("Let's get to the golf course!") that there is no strong sentiment for another point of view ("Let's spend the day improving expense account reporting procedures!").

In neither case is there the basis for much flexibility.

If your situation skews the two sides toward either extreme—adamant hostility or universal agreement—think twice before wasting too much energy in negotiation.

tip   **Command the Middle Ground**   Where opinions are frozen and polarized, you will spend an inordinate amount of time trying to build even a modest consensus just to deviate from the status quo—let alone discuss matters of substance. On the other hand, if you find yourself toward the middle, where there are more diverse opinions and approaches, you have room to operate. For a negotiator, this is the optimal place to be, because here you find the most options to explore.

HOW MUCH POWER DOES EACH SIDE HAVE?

In order to have the parity required to negotiate, both sides must possess enough autonomous power to give them some bargaining chips.

Does the other side have the autonomy to make an independent decision or are they under someone else's commands? If they're part of a bureaucracy or an organization, are they sufficiently empowered to exercise discretion in how they choose to implement policy? Are they the decision makers?

If the answer is yes, you can confidently proceed with a negotiation. If your answer is no, can you get to somebody with sufficient independence and rank? A second no bodes ill because you will have to invest considerable effort just to get to the point of initiating the formal negotiation. The other side will be responsible for representing your position to their superiors. A lot will probably be lost in the translation.

What Are You Trying to Accomplish?

If you have a single fixed objective with limited acceptable alternatives, your range of action is tightly restricted. If, for example, nothing less than a full scholarship to Harvard will satisfy you, you don't have many options. It's tough to structure a win-win situation when you're backed into a corner. On the other hand, if you would welcome even partial aid to any university with a good science program, there are many ways to proceed.

When there are multiple ways to achieve the same objective, you possess enough flexibility to be able to negotiate. Negotiating with a taxi driver on the price of a long drive is much easier at midday when you could take another cab, the bus, or the train, than it would be at midnight, when you're stranded and there's only one cab.

What Else Is on Your Screen?

Are you prepared to invest the necessary attention to this negotiation? That may mean hours on the telephone, writing lots of correspondence, or maybe conducting research to find evidence to back up your position. Does it make sense to pursue this negotiation in the context of your other responsibilities? Again, the more emphatically you answer yes, the stronger your negotiating position.

 Don't Waste Your Silver Bullets Pick your shots carefully. Test the waters first.

TESTING THE WATERS

Here's a trick to help you discover if the other side is primed to deal. Make a *trial request*. Gauging the nature of the response gives you a better sense of whether you're in a favorable negotiation situation.

For example, suppose you're shopping for a home theater system. You want to know how eager the store is to make the sale, what kind of add-ons and perks you can get, and whether the salesman is empowered to negotiate. As you listen to the salesman's pitch, float up a low-risk trial balloon. "By the way," you might say, "I'll want delivery at no charge and the driver to install the home theater on the second floor of my home." How does the salesman react? If he abruptly answers "That's not how we do it" and treats you like a bumpkin, you know this is not a good negotiation situation. If, on the other hand, he takes your request seriously (even if he doesn't agree immediately), he'll likely have flexibility to work with other demands, such as price, service, installation, and so on.

Making a request embodies considerable power. It ups the ante of the exchange, informing the other side that you are not passive and that they are not in complete control. It serves to redefine the stakes. By shaking up habitual patterns of behavior and thought, you encourage creative problem solving. By voicing a demand, you communicate that you are aware of your options. All of these factors enhance your ability to engage in productive negotiation.

MAKING THE TRIAL REQUEST: A PRACTICE EXERCISE

As you become a more experienced negotiator, you'll become more adept at making the trial request. In order to speed up the process and help you feel more comfortable performing what can first feel like an unacceptably difficult and assertive act, do the following: During the next week pose several trial requests just to get the feel for how it's done. Do this in your personal relationships, at work, and in a store. Your goal is not to make a deal but rather to sharpen up your "negotiation antennae" and see the effect that a request has on an interaction.

1. My practice request in a store was:

   _____

   The other side's response was:

   _____

   Based on this response, was the situation favorable for negotiation?

   _____

2. My practice request in a personal relationship was:

   _____

   The other side's response was:

   _____

   Based on this response, was the situation favorable for negotiation?

   _____

3. My practice request at work was:

   _____

   The other side's response was:

   _____

   Based on this response, was the situation favorable for negotiation?

   _____

In this lesson you learned how to recognize an opportune negotiating situation.

THE "SCIENCE" OF EXCHANGE VS. THE "ART" OF THE BARGAIN

In this lesson you learn to combine objective planning with emotional sensitivity.

Some people would have us believe that human behavior is purely rational. (You can bet, however, that these people aren't negotiators!) Perhaps many exchanges are measured by the objectivity of dollars and cents, but that's not all they are made of. As any good salesperson knows, in the dialogue of persuasion, people are swayed by hopes and dreams, by ideals and fears.

Think of a negotiation as a sale that you are trying to make—it is part exchange, part bargain. To close the deal, you must consider both the head and the heart.

The *head* represents the objective and rational side of an exchange. As discussed later, the key to this part of the equation is thorough planning. You need answers to these fundamental exchange questions in order to properly plan:

- What do you want from the exchange?
- What does the other party want from the exchange?

- When do you want it?

- How much will you give up for it?

- How much will the other party sacrifice?

There is another side of the equation as well, the artistic sensibilities. This part of the equation eludes hard, measurable answers. Instead, you must rely on your sensitivity, intuition, and ability to empathize with others. Consider these questions:

- How do you feel about the situation? How does the other party feel about the situation?

- How do you both feel about each other?

- How do you both feel about the importance of success or the consequences of failure?

tip   **Successful Persuasion**   In order to persuade others, they must be tempted, motivated, and closed just like a customer in a sale. Your point of view is the product you are selling. Successful persuasion requires you to appeal to emotions as well as to facts and figures.

APPRAISING THE EMOTIONAL COMPONENT

In forming an approach to a negotiation, remember to take into account the psychological implications of personality. Often, a negotiation will succeed or fail not because of material considerations but because the emotional context of the dialogue becomes hopelessly muddled. Instead of working collaboratively to achieve a win-win scenario, the sides find themselves at loggerheads.

When the chemistry between the two sides goes sour, it may not matter that objective conditions are still favorable. If the emotional foundations for a bargain have fallen apart, the bargain is most likely doomed.

A PSYCHOLOGICAL INVENTORY OF INTENT

Before you enter into the dialogue of persuasion, try to determine what makes your negotiating partner tick. Clarify in your own mind how they may respond to different approaches.

In terms of general goals and objectives, does the other side tend to be clear or confused? Forthright or cagey? Is the other side open about expressing emotion or closed? Outspoken or reserved?

In relationships, is the other side outgoing or introverted? A social extrovert or a loner? Significantly attached to another or single?

When the other side skews towards the warm, affable, sociable profile, you can feel confident in broaching intimacy, sharing confidences, communicating instinctively, and encouraging the bonding of friendship.

When the other side skews toward guarded, precise, and solitary, you will derive more success by sticking to a more formal, distant, impersonal approach.

A PSYCHOLOGICAL INVENTORY OF PROCESS

After the dialogue of persuasion begins, the interaction takes on a higher level of complexity. You are building on the core of personality, compounded with the particularities of the negotiation. It is even more important at this point to be at-tuned to the art of the deal. Consider these questions:

- Is the other side temperamentally shy or bold? Do you have to draw them out or cool them down?

- Is the other side receptive to creative solutions or are they more comfortable with established rules and procedures? Will they agree to a spontaneous inno-vation or do they require a previously accepted pre-cedent?

- Does the other side tend to communicate through direct dialogue or do they prefer hints and indirect signals? Are they more likely to respond to direct confrontation or subtle implications?

 Path Markings   The art in a negotiation is being able to read the emotional trailmarkers along the way and becoming skillful in hacking away the brush blocking the path to your destination.

Protecting Yourself Against Your Own Worst Impulses

Often you'll find that the other side seems hopelessly hard-headed and resistant to persuasion. This is frustrating for all negotiators. Guard yourself against impatience when facing this mind-numbing style. It's all too easy to attack.

Resist the impulse in such circumstances to attribute bad faith to their obstinacy, even if they resist your point of view.

What if you have to negotiate with a tight-lipped, supercilious egotist who looks down his nose at you? What are your options? Before you conclude that you're dealing with a certified creep, consider the emotional side of the equation.

Re-examine your tactics, particularly your approach. Have you been too aggressive? Have you overestimated his capability to reason from precedent or to draw logical connections? Have you underestimated his need to have everything spelled out?

Equal parts science and art maintain the momentum of a negotiation. Techniques and methodologies prepare you to get what you want. Nimble sensitivity and empathy provide the finesse to keep the train heading down the track.

USING THE NON-OFFENSIVE OFFENSE

Have you ever watched a great artist draw? The lines flow effortlessly from the pencil. A mark here, a bit of shadow there, and out of the pieces suddenly emerges a coherent image. An artistic negotiation works the same way—a subtle suggestion here; a direct request there. A small concession at exactly the right moment can seal the deal.

The art of the bargain is to achieve your objectives with such deft precision and economy of effort that the other side, rather than resisting the process, contributes to it. In the same way, a black-belt warrior uses his opponent's own force to win through subtle deflection.

As with any complex process, there are general principles that contribute to a winning style, but no rules etched in stone. The better grounded you are in the fundamentals, the more you can improvise by using a personal approach.

Brilliant solutions appear when you go outside the box—beyond the restrictive boundaries of the rules you have learned. To get outside the box requires both a scientist's discipline and an artist's flair. On the one hand, it requires doing your homework in advance; on the other it requires intuitive insight into what makes your potential customer tick.

In this lesson you learned to combine objective planning with emotional sensitivity.

LESSON

5

THE SPIRIT OF A NEGOTIATOR: ENERGIZING ACTION

In this lesson you learn the correct attitude to direct the flow of a negotiation.

A master negotiator is a modern-day version of the mythic warrior who defeated his enemies through the strength of his skill and the purity of his power. If King Arthur were alive today, his Knights of the Round Table might study negotiation instead of archery.

Energizing a Situation   Directing the flow of action or managing a negotiation process.

Keep Your Eye on the Ball   Regardless of specific objectives, your main goal in any negotiation remains the same: to direct the flow of action so it moves toward mutual goals. Strategies and tactics may differ from one negotiation to another—your intention is always to manage the process toward a positive outcome.

SAY WHAT YOU MEAN, MEAN WHAT YOU SAY

A problem with warriors is that they can lose sight of their mission and become attached to battle for its own sake. The same goes for negotiators. Instead of energizing a phased process of resolution, a negotiator can sometimes become absorbed in competition for its own sake. Rather than focusing on a goal, the negotiation deteriorates into accusations and rebuttals. Conflict becomes an end in itself.

Apart from the wounded feelings, the real danger is that positions previously flexible and open to compromise become fixed in concrete as a result of impulsive statements made in anger. As stated in *The Tao of Negotiation* (Joel Edelman and Mary Beth Crain, Harper Business, 1994; p. 84), "In disputes, because emotions are usually exaggerated, wants often become exaggerated as well, escalating from mere desires into demands and legal 'rights'."

At the end of the day, the consequences of such charged exchanges are not normally a mutually advantageous settlement.

ENERGIZING THE SITUATION

Energizing the situation does not mean dictating the end results. Directing the flow is about commitment to process, not the celebration of your own importance.

Inflated estimates of who we are and what we deserve—those manifestations of excessive ego that psychologists call *delusions of grandeur*—are constant threats to the process.

The heroic warrior knows that a true negotiation is not a personality dispute. It is about substantive, objective issues, not a means to prove prowess, enhance self-esteem, obliterate a rival, or be sucked in to the other person's bouts of emotion and ego.

Separate your objective needs from your subjective wants. In a negotiation, you are dealing with external issues—position, money, authority, commodities. Although the temptation often exists to confuse matters, achieving these demands has nothing to do with your subjective desires for love, respect, compassion, and the whole range of deep-seated needs.

Ask for what you want and want what you ask for. Don't turn your objectives into coded demands for acting out past emotional problems that the present negotiation cannot possibly resolve.

 Stay Cool Under Fire   When you sense your ego about to erupt, ask yourself: What am I feeling? What am I thinking? Where are these feelings and thoughts coming from? Do they have anything to do with this negotiation? Will they help or hinder my ability to manage the process?

UNDERSTANDING THE RULES TO ENERGIZE ACTION

Remember that to energize action is to direct the flow of action or to manage a negotiation process. These rules help you to do just that:

1. Say what you believe, and believe what you say.

2. Guard your credibility; it is the single most valuable element you bring to the negotiation.

3. Offer your potential customer true value; don't try to hard-sell shoddy merchandise.

4. Cultivate strength without becoming hard.

5. Practice the three F's: flexibility, fairness, and follow-through.

In this lesson you learned the correct attitude to direct the flow of a negotiation.

THE RIGHT STUFF: THE HABITS OF SUCCESS

In this lesson you learn the importance of planning, listening, and timing.

Skillful negotiation is a learned behavior—you have to learn how to walk before you can run.

Like the pleasure of caviar or scotch, an appreciation for negotiation, too, is something of an acquired taste. It doesn't come with the first experience. Indeed, in the beginning, bargaining may make you feel painfully self-conscious and uncomfortable. That's to be expected. Stick with it. After a few tries, as the habits become second nature, you'll find great satisfaction (and considerable benefits) in being a skillful negotiator.

HABIT #1: PLAN YOUR WORK AND WORK YOUR PLAN

To expand on a theme already introduced, the single most important phase of the process occurs before the face-to-face part of a negotiation even begins. This is *your* preparation.

The importance of preparing fully cannot be overstated ("Luck," as the great baseball executive Branch Rickey observed, "is the residue of design"). Yet it is stunning how often even seasoned pros will try to wing their way through a negotiation without having done their homework. Quick wit and social skills may partially carry the day, but with adequate preparation the results are even greater.

Pay Attention to the Details   As a useful rule of thumb, you should invest as much time in planning for a negotiation as will be spent in the actual face-to-face negotiation.

Americans' impatient spirit and love of instant gratification makes us tend to rush into a venture before the preparation has been adequately laid ("Ready, Fire, Aim!"). The Japanese, by contrast, will spend forever planning an undertaking right down to the most unlikely contingency. They take an eternity to get started but once underway more than make up the difference in rapid, hassle-free implementation. This willingness to prepare is often cited as one reason they're so adept at bringing products quickly to market.

To be a skilled negotiator, you must be willing to pay for the prep work. If you retain no other idea from this book, remember this one: There is no alternative in a successful negotiation to planning your strategy and tactics.

Put Your Plan in Writing   Before you enter a negotiation, make your plan. Write it down. Share it with your advisers. Make adjustments as circumstances change, but keep it fresh in your mind.

Sometimes you will be negotiating for large amounts of money and big prizes. Sometimes your objectives will be

much simpler. Either way, the key is to know where you want
to end up and how you intend to get there.

tip   **Define Your Goal**   If you don't know what you're
looking for, you'll never know when you find it. If
you don't know where you're going, you'll never
arrive at your destination.

HABIT #2: STOP, LOOK, AND LISTEN

A skilled negotiator is a lot like a sponge, absorbing every con-
ceivable scrap of information pertaining to the environment.
To accomplish this, you don't need fancy spy gear. The most
important tools are already attached on either side of your
head: your ears!

The way to obtain maximum useful information is by *non-
judgmental observation*. Simply put, this means listening with
an open mind, without the set of habitual filters we all use to
screen what we hear. When we don't listen with an open
mind, we attribute motives to the other side that they may not
have, hear threats and promises they may not intend, distort
messages to reinforce the "reality" we already believe rather
than the view they are presenting.

Non-judgmental observation enables us to listen for pure content. This will help immeasurably in understanding the other
side's position and in formulating our own responses to their
point of view.

tip

The Zen of Listening To practice non-judgmental observation, the principles recommended by Zen mystics are useful:

Listen to the words more than the person speaking them.

Listen to the content of thought more than the words being spoken.

Listen to the deepest meaning of intent more than the contours of thought.

Listen to your own internal experience more than the meaning of intent.

HABIT #3: SEPARATE THE PERSON FROM THE PROBLEM

The bad news is that this is easier said than done. The good news is that you can learn how! Disjunction—separating the person from the problem—enables you to maximize the usefulness of your relationship regardless of how you feel about the other side.

Of course, feelings matter and affect the conduct of the negotiation itself. Blame, hurt, envy, and pride are all real. The key, however, is to refuse to let hostile personal responses sour a positive working relationship.

It is your responsibility, as a master negotiator controlling the flow of the process, to take unconditional responsibility for keeping substantive and relationship issues separate. Figuring out a strategy to do this is part of your preparation. During the negotiation itself, one of your critical tasks is to stay focused on the substantive issues regardless of how the other side behaves.

tip   **Anticipate Frustration**   As part of your preparation, compile a list of the other side's personality traits that annoy you. Get them all down on paper. Visualize yourself in negotiation as the other side displays each trait. Experience your feelings. Feel your response. Consult this list before each session and repeat the exercise. Use up your irritation in this exercise rather than in the actual encounter.

HABIT #4: DEFINE YOUR INTENTION

A negotiation is a journey of measured steps. Sometimes each phase is distinctly marked with a clear mile post, sometimes the territory blurs together.

The first phase is the *information gathering* phase. You are learning all you can about the situation, your options, and your fellow negotiator. During this phase, your purpose is to listen more than you talk. Your intention is to get answers to specific questions you have formulated during the course of your preparation.

The next phase is the *issue resolution* phase, when each side offers their demands and poses their initial responses. In this stage, your intention is to further dialogue for the sake of clarification. You do this by offering good faith information and responding to objections and suggestions from the other side as each seeks more fully to define the points of disagreement. During this phase, it is still too early to try to reconcile differences.

The final phase is the *decision making* phase. This is when horse-trading takes place, when the final details are hammered out. In this phase, your intention is to avoid making unnecessary concessions without violating the spirit of a win-win agreement. During this phase you will be "tough without being hard" and "flexible without being weak."

In this lesson you learned the importance of planning, listening, and timing.

PATIENCE AND PREPARATION

In this lesson you learn the tactics of patience and preparation.

Trying to copy another negotiator's style is a hopeless endeavor. There is no single model. Some styles are rough-and-tumble like pushcart peddlers, others are as elegant as a custom-tailored Saville Row suit. Whether your preference is for no-nonsense straight talk or smooth diplomatic polish, however, the keys to accomplishment are something you can emulate. They are patience and preparation, the two hallmarks of every successful negotiator.

PATIENCE: KEEPING COOL UNDER PRESSURE

Patience first. If you can outwait the other side, you can usually out-maneuver them. Whether the negotiators are two world-class players or you and your three-year-old struggling over one more bedtime story, the first side to blink usually loses.

In the broadest sense, patience involves more than mere physical endurance. With respect to negotiation, patience requires a target, timetable, and tactics. Staying power comes from steady focus. "I have seen countless negotiations fall apart because of impatience," notes a seasoned observer, "but I can't recall a negotiation that ended unhappily because of the shrewd, calculated exercise of patience."

PREPARATION: DOING YOUR HOMEWORK

Regardless of what you are trying to accomplish—buy cheap or sell high, convince a significant other to marry you or exit from your life, receive a promotion or acquire a client's business—the planning process is the same. In this stage, you must answer the following questions:

1. What do I want?

2. How much is it worth to me to obtain this objective?

3. Whom must I convince to say yes for this to happen?

 Plan to Win   Effective preparation requires comprehensive information, option development, and commitment to a plan of attack.

Great coaches know that one of their most important jobs is to get their team mentally prepared to win. The same goes with negotiation. Answering these questions gets your head in the right place so you can play to the utmost of your ability.

WHAT DO I WANT?

Sounds simple, right? You want a new house or for your daughter to obey you or to buy a company. These are specific demands. But when you begin to explore the interests that underlie them, you usually discover a subtext of desire in which deciding what you want isn't always so crystal clear.

Specific Demand   The object you want.

Interest   The underlying cause that manifests itself in the demand.

For example, your child wants an automobile. The car is the specific demand. The interest is the child's desire to have independence to come and go.

To determine what you want, make a list beginning with the most specific, concrete objects and work through to the more subjective.

For example, say you're in the market to buy a house. List your priorities in declining importance: Style? Neighborhood? Size? Condition? Then think of other things you want: Flower gardens? Friendly neighbors? Walking distance to the local coffee bar?

Then you might consider such questions as: Will my family be happy? Will my business colleagues and clients be impressed? Will my mother-in-law stop complaining to my wife about how all her friends' daughters married better?

Or say you're the father of a teenage daughter who is insisting against your objections that she be allowed to sleep over at her boyfriend's house. What do you want? To protect her from a compromising situation? To have her accept your values? To maintain control over her actions? To guard her from emotional injury? To have her stay at home so she can do her chores and homework? Would other desires be to maintain an open, honest relationship with her? To retain her respect? To show her you love her? Maybe even to demonstrate to her and her boyfriend that you're still the alpha male?

Or say you're the CEO of a big company thinking about buying another company. What do you want? To enhance shareholder value? To grow revenue? To implement a strategic plan? Perhaps to make your company too big for a competitor to buy out? To earn a bonus for making the acquisition? To protect the security of your job? Perhaps to make yourself become more important in the eyes of the board of directors?

The point of this exercise is to begin with a hard-core want list, the bread-and-butter specific demands. Then ask yourself, "Why do I want these? For what purpose?" This second order of questions helps identify the broader interests which underlie what at first might seem specific, non-negotiable demands.

As you'll likely discover, the satisfaction of the general interests is often more important to you than what at first seemed to be a specific demand (for example, you want a certain kind of house to get your mother-in-law off your back; you want your daughter to obey her parents; you want to make the acquisition to deflect the criticism of office rivals).

Interests, unlike *arbitrary positions,* can be fulfilled in a variety of ways. Once you identify your interests, you'll be better able to think of a variety of demands to satisfy them. These options provide you with alternatives to invoke during the negotiation.

How Much Is It Worth?

Valuation is arbitrary. One man's meat is another man's poison. During your preparation period, figure out what your different demands are worth to you. Prioritize them according to an index that you find useful, such as money, time, energy, opportunity cost, uniqueness, or difficulty to obtain or replace.

By establishing values, you are better able to compare the worth of alternative solutions. When you enter into the later phases of the negotiation, knowing in advance the value you attach enables you to bargain with more shrewdness.

As part of your strategy, decide what you're going to pursue and what you're willing to give up if the price is too high. (Of course, don't share this information about either valuation or priorities with the other side!)

Then make a similar index for the other side. Try to identify their demands and interests, then determine how much you think they value them. The same object can have strongly different values to either side even within the same negotiation. (Think of the game of Monopoly: any property is much more valuable when it's the missing link in a monopoly than when it's the only property owned of that color.)

Let's say you decide to buy your daughter a high-quality used auto that has been carefully maintained, and you are willing to pay a premium for safety. The seller, on the other hand, wants a new image for herself and is tired of her dull, stodgy, "unsexy" car. In this negotiation, your valuation and the seller's valuation of the same object are likely to be very different (giving you a good bargaining advantage).

WHOM MUST I CONVINCE TO SAY YES?

On the surface, this is another no-brainer. The person to persuade is sitting across the table, right? Not necessarily!

As you proceed through your preparation, you will begin to notice that there are often hidden chains of command and circles within circles.

For starters, it is always a good ploy to present yourself as having to report to another person who will make the final decision. Invoking the need to gain supplemental approval from "the boss" (who is not present) frees you up to respond in light of the understanding that any decision made at the table is subject to change because somebody else has the last word.

Always Have a Boss   Even if you don't have a boss or superior, in a negotiation it is to your advantage to pretend that you do. Knowing that you will have to sell your deal to somebody else usually tempers the other side and moderates their demands.

In preparing yourself, conduct an inventory of the other side:

1. Is there pressure on them to do this deal or can they walk away without any damage?

2. Is the other side empowered to take a risk?

3. Does the other side require immediate results?

4. Has the other side ever done a deal like this before? What were the results? Is the precedent favorable/ unfavorable to you?

5. Is the other side an experienced negotiator? If so, what kinds of strategies are they likely to employ?

Always assume that you're dealing with a pro who is sharper than you, especially when she's playing dumb and simple. But if the other side really is an amateur, be diplomatic when you say no.

In this lesson you learned the tactics of patience and preparation.

PERSUASION

In this lesson you learn how to persuade different personality types, provide authority to your position, and cleverly weaken the other side's position.

Preparation is the backstage part of negotiation. It's where you prop the set and cue the lights and write the script. This all occurs out of sight. Persuasion is the action that occurs before an audience. It's the main event—the give-and-take that gets you to "yes."

IDENTIFYING CHARACTER CATEGORIES: "TO THINE OWN SELF BE TRUE"

Roadblocks emerge when dialogue breaks down. Obviously, no opportunity for persuasion exists without discourse. It is particularly important to keep the channels of communication free-flowing during the stressful moments that accompany negotiation.

You and the other side might not be able to talk for several reasons. Sometimes it's because you're stuck on a specific issue. Sometimes, however, this impasse has little to do with content but occurs because the communication process itself has become jammed with static.

How does this happen? As each side expresses demands, communication can shift gears from "dialogue" to "self-protection." If one side feels threatened and under attack, they are likely to revert to behavior that obstructs honest exchange. Obstructionist style falls into four dominant categories, explained briefly here (but covered fully in *The Tao of Negotiation*, by Joel Edelman and Mary Beth Crain). By understanding these character categories in advance, you will be better prepared to recognize and dismantle them when they show up in the negotiation (and also avoid falling into one of the roles yourself):

- **Attackers/Defenders:** Their style is belligerent and aggressive because they think the other side is the enemy. Attackers/defenders think that the other side is out to destroy them. They perceive no middle ground. They must have everything their own way.

- **Accommodators:** Their style is motivated by fear and a sense of powerlessness. They believe that conflict is worse than abandoning their position so they give in rather than fight for what they believe. But in doing this, they perceive themselves to be victims. Not only do they not accomplish what they want, they also resent their own role as martyr.

- **Avoiders:** Their style is motivated by the need to deny a reality so painful that it cannot be admitted. Rather than engage in dialogue over an issue, they deny that a problem exists (this is the classic pattern of substance abusers and co-dependents). By refusing to involve themselves in real issues, they are unable to engage in the honest communication that leads to substantive negotiation.

- **Stalematers:** Their style is motivated by self-righteous insistence that there is only one side to a misunderstanding—their own. They are more concerned with insisting that they are right than resolving a dispute. They remain entrenched and unyielding (often refusing to take a meeting with the other side or even acknowledge any legitimacy to the other side's position).

When one of these patterns results in an impasse, you must immobilize the obstruction in order to resume a dialogue.

- Seek to free an attacker from the corner where they feel trapped; assure them of the reliability of your good will and intention to honor a mutually beneficial agreement.

- Encourage an accommodator to focus on what they want for themselves; encourage them in the dialogue to formulate issues and not simply back down or give in.

- Clearly acknowledge the legitimacy of a stalemater's point of view and your willingness to respond to the substance of the problem; do not debate "right and wrong" or who is to blame.

- Create a safe, accepting space for an avoider to acknowledge that a problem exists and structure your dialogue so they have to confront the issue.

PERSUADING BY SKEPTICISM: "SAYS WHO?"

Persuasion involves creating a story line to support a position.

Your goal is to weave the facts and implications of a situation into a narrative that makes the other side understand the legitimacy of what you want and makes them willing to accept your demands. Facts, figures, and precedents continually enter into the presentation to make your point.

Like facts in a trial, a persuasive argument is woven from a multitude of assumptions. And like a shrewd attorney, you want to present your assumptions in the strongest possible light and not accept the other side's claims on face value.

Persuasion by skepticism is a powerful tool for undermining the narrative power of the other side's facts, figures, and premises. You do this not by debating the accuracy but rather questioning as neutrally as possible the source of the assumption. Without challenging the accuracy or correctness of the other party's positions, continually ask how they were arrived at.

For example, if the other side quotes a certain price, ask where they got the number. Don't object, just inquire as to its rationale. Or if you're negotiating an employment contract and it's assumed you'll receive two weeks of vacation, ask how this policy was arrived at (later in the process you'll ask for four weeks). If the other side wants to schedule a Saturday meeting that is inconvenient for you, ask why.

There are many deal points in every negotiation process. Each side wants to decide each of them as unilaterally as possible; this lets them write the rules of the negotiation. Your mission is to spot those unilateral calls, oblige the other side to explain them, and then, if you don't accept, offer an alternative.

Your simple act of requesting justification is itself a powerful defense against their presumption.

Whenever a statement of fact is made in a negotiation, or an assumption is put forward as though it were obvious or non-controversial, let the warning bell ring in your head and ask yourself "Says who?"

Going Beyond Stubbornness: Measuring Fairness

An external standard of measurement provides a basis for resolving differences of opinion. It affords a level of objectivity that is hard to challenge effectively. These rationales of legitimacy constitute an important element in the successful negotiator's persuasion arsenal.

Legitimacy   How you justify a demand. If your only argument is "I want it!", you'll have to pay a high premium to get the other side to agree. Because many negotiations have to be taken back to a third party for approval, it is important that the legitimacy of the agreement be apparent when it comes time for the boss to ratify the results.

What are the different ways to legitimize a demand?

Precedent is reasoning from prior example. Lawyers, for example, cite precedent judgments to prior similar cases when they make an argument. What examples can you find in comparable situations that resemble the issues you are negotiating? The more examples, the better. Precedent is the single most powerful legitimization.

Citing judgment by a third party referee is a high standard of legitimacy to win a negotiation. It is always to your advantage to support your demands with backup evidence from impartial or eminent sources. Expert testimony is hard to challenge.

Accepted principles and practices are strong planks in a platform. If you can demonstrate how your demands are normal and usual practice (for example, new employees of your rank and experience receive four weeks vacation throughout your industry), the other side will have difficulty resisting the legitimacy of your claims.

Last, but by no means least, are examples of actions taken by the other side in comparable circumstances. If you know what the other side asked for or conceded in the past, they'll be hard pressed to argue with your logic in asking for the same treatment.

UNDERSTANDING THE VIRTUE OF PERSISTENCE

Refusing to give up can prove to be the most compelling persuasion of all.

Just as in the folk tale, in most negotiations it is the slow and steady tortoise who wins the race, not the hare, who bursts out of the gate only to run out of steam.

The persuasion of your point of view prevails over time through a steady, determined approach in which you simply refuse to accept the other side's "no" for the final answer.

You don't have to be confrontational and argumentative. When they say "no," just smile and agree with their logic. ("I can see why you feel this way. In your position, I probably would feel the same way. But let me point out a few more reasons to justify my position that you might not be familiar with.")

Persistence means you keep charge over your emotions. Don't flare up. Don't get angry. Always be agreeable. Don't worry if the other party thinks they're in control. You know that you are! Being agreeable and accommodating is not the same thing as being weak.

The persuasion of persistence is like inflicting the Chinese water torture on the other side. You state your position, listen to the other side's responses, repeat your position in light of their responses, listen to their new responses, state your position again, and so on and so on and so on.

Let the other side range in temper, and you keep your cool. They will exhaust themselves by the end, frustrated and angry and guilty of bad judgment. You, on the other hand, will have steadily adhered to your tactical offensive.

Slow and Steady Wins the Race   Negotiators don't retreat! They build momentum.

Two steps forward, one step back, one step sideways carries the day!

In this lesson you learned how to persuade different personality types, provide authority to your position, and cleverly weaken the other side's position.

ASSERTIVE
LISTENING

In this lesson you learn the importance of hearing the other side so that you will be able to exercise maximum leverage.

Newcomers to negotiation tend to focus on the "talk" side. They direct most of their attention to what they want and defending their demands. Seasoned negotiators, however, know that listening can be more important than talking. Hearing the other party is as important as making sure they hear you.

 Keep Your Ears Open   You don't learn by talking—you already know what you're going to say. You learn by listening.

Some of the most effective negotiators speak the least. Successful negotiation is not measured by "air time," by long-winded oratory, or by verbally bullying the other side into submission. It's measured by saying the right words at the right time to exercise maximum leverage. Locating the leverage points that exist in any dialogue is the consummate negotiation skill.

How do you identify them? By assertively listening to the other side.

Assertive Listening   Listening actively, which requires mental participation. The assertive listener monitors what he hears, constructing a "dictionary" of the language the other party uses so he can comprehend their fullest meaning and speak to them in a way they understand. Assertive listening is not a passive process; it is a practiced skill that enables you to hear the underlying ideas of the other side.

BE HERE NOW

We've all had this painful experience. You're with somebody important—perhaps at a job interview or on a romantic date or even with your companion at a dinner party. You want to make a good impression. So instead of listening to their half of the conversation, as they talk you worry about what you're going to say next. As a result, you don't even hear them. And when your turn does come, instead of exercising leverage on the dialogue, your remarks fall with a heavy thud. It's as if two separate discussions are going on, conducted in the form of monologues. This is the opposite of assertive listening.

A technique practiced by Zen masters can be useful in helping you avoid this pitfall. As you participate in a negotiation, allow your mind to relax and focus on being present—being in the here and now. That means that when the other side speaks, the "hear and now" act is to listen to their words (and not focus on what you should say next). One way to do this is to mind your breath—monitor yourself inhaling and exhaling, which settles and calms the mind.

When we drift out of the moment, we tend to get lost in our own prejudices, attitudes, judgments, and preconceptions. Instead of hearing the other side as they are, we end up recycling our own inner noise. Active listening means to be present and responsive in the moment, not to be trapped in a memory or an expectation.

You don't have to be a mystic to refine your listening skills, but you can borrow the concept of "mindfulness" from several millennia of Eastern thought to speed you on your way. In his book *Wherever You Go There You Are* (Hyperion, 1994), Jon Kabat-Zinn says that "Mindfulness means paying attention in a particular way: on purpose, in the present moment, and nonjudgmentally. This kind of attention nurtures greater awareness, clarity, and acceptance of present-moment reality."

PREPARING TO LISTEN: THE SKILL SET

As with any skill, you become a better listener over time. Attentive experience refines your performance. The skills are not particularly difficult; keeping yourself open and mindful is the tricky part. Use the following techniques to learn better listening skills:

1. Cue in to "tip-offs": We all have certain phrases and expressions we use to express intense feelings of joy, anger, agreement, distrust. For example, when hippies from the sixties said "Far out!" they were sharing a sentiment of approval (much like the current use of "cool").

Today, when a twenty-something says "Whatever," they are dismissing the importance of a topic as if to say "No difference; it doesn't matter, so get on with it."

As you practice assertive listening, learn to take inventory of the other party's linguistic cues. How do they express modest interest? Strong disapproval? Frustration? Excitement? Hostility? Acceptance?

2. Identify the hot buttons: All issues in a negotiation are not created equal. In gaining and exercising leverage, it is to your advantage to be able to differentiate the other side's key interests from their less important interests. Although a skilled negotiator tries to hide this from you (since she doesn't want you to know the "deal breakers" from the "deal makers" until the horse trading starts), you can often learn what's really important from her language.

3. How do they "frame" or present their positions? Try to hear the way they perceive the issues. For example, suppose your landlord unexpectedly raises your rent beyond what you think is fair. You negotiate for a reduction. He agrees that you are a good tenant but complains he has no option because of rising utility costs. You hear the importance of utility costs and agree to pay the increase, which is significantly less than the proposed rent increase.

In this lesson you learned the importance of hearing the other side so that you will be able to exercise maximum leverage.

10

Winning Ways: Your Personal Inventory

In this lesson you learn how to evaluate your negotiating personality style.

In this chapter, you evaluate yourself in terms of four basic personality characteristics that influence your skill as a negotiator. Consider each question carefully before you answer. The intent is to stimulate your self-awareness. Take your time.

Directions: Circle the letter of the response that best applies to you. Although you may feel that none of the options fits you perfectly, pick the one that is closest to how you perceive yourself. Be honest.

PLANNING

A. I feel that I am a very disciplined planner. I think through almost everything I do. I make detailed lists and always follow through on them. I set concrete goals for myself every day.

B. I make lists for myself, but not in every instance. I possess a general vision for what I want to accomplish, but sometimes I get bogged down in details. When things get hectic, I plunge ahead on intuition.

C. I rarely if ever make lists. I believe over-planning gets in the way of spontaneity and real creativity. I take things the way they come.

DIRECT REQUESTS

A. I almost always know what I want and am not shy about asking for it. I don't worry that I may hurt the feelings of others. A request is strictly business.

B. I know what I want when it's important to me. Sometimes I don't know what I want (or particularly care) because it isn't that important. When I think something is important, I make my needs known; when I don't, I may seem vague because communicating my needs isn't important to me at that time. I expect others to be sensitive to my needs the same way I am sensitive to theirs and I get frustrated when people don't understand what I am asking for.

C. I think, in most cases, that every problem has many solutions and that one is as good as another. I go with the flow. I don't want my requests to impose on others. I don't like people to have to say no to me. I avoid potentially charged conversations.

PATIENCE

A. I never get upset with people with whom I do business. It takes me a while to get involved in a project or with a committee, but once I do I stay with it until the end.

B. I can stick to a goal as long as it is realistic to me. But when the odds are bad or nil, my enthusiasm wanes. I finish only the important things that I start.

C. I tend to get discouraged when things don't happen my way. I don't like the tension of uncertainty. I need gratification quickly or I move on to something else.

LISTENING SKILLS

A. People seek me out when they have problems they need to discuss. When I am in a conversation, I listen "behind" the words in order to understand what the other person really means. I do not feel as if I must always be talking in a conversation. I often remember little facts about people.

B. I enjoy conversations and often have long talks with people. When I am with somebody interesting, I listen. I normally dominate the conversation. I can often predict what somebody will say before they say it.

C. I feel that conversations exist to accomplish a goal. If you keep to the point, people say what they want. I take people at face value most of the time. I don't try to figure out where people are coming from in a conversation.

HOW TO RATE YOURSELF

There are four key personal areas that shape your success as a negotiator: Planning, Making Direct Requests, Patience, and Listening Skills. Whatever your natural predisposition and talents, you can train yourself to do better in each area.

Here's how to score yourself:

> For each A you circled, add 3.

> For each B you circled, add 2.

> For each C you circled, add 1.

A score between 10–12 means that you possess the basic personal skills to be an astute negotiator. You plan, are patient, listen well, and make direct requests. You start out with an edge in a negotiation because of these skills.

A score between 6–9 means that you have strength in some areas, but you need to establish more consistency in your approach. There is a weakness somewhere in your "total negotiating personal style." Identify those areas (where you scored 1 or 2) and pay special attention to them.

A score of less than 6 means you need to exercise firm discipline throughout the negotiation process. Your natural personality is not that of a negotiator. But this does not mean you cannot become a good negotiator. By knowing your weaknesses in advance, you are better prepared to correct them.

In this lesson you learned how to evaluate your negotiating personality style.

11

THE NEGOTIATION PARADIGM: POWER × TIME × INFORMATION

In this lesson you learn to evaluate the factors of power, time, and information that comprise the negotiation context.

Now you're ready to consider specific cases. In this section, you learn how to plan for a specific negotiation in more detailed terms. In considering all these elements, you are defining the context of the negotiation.

Every negotiation has elements that are both unique and universal—aspects that pertain only to this specific issue and aspects that pertain to every situation. By establishing the context, you can identify the universal aspects. The interplay of these elements—both unique and universal—has a large role in shaping the outcome.

Negotiation Paradigm The context of a negotiation. It is the surrounding system within which the negotiation develops. This paradigm is composed of three elements: power, time, and information.

POWER

Every situation contains diverse elements of power. Your power elements are the chips you use to make your deals. It helps to imagine a scale: On one end are your power assets (formal authority, strength of reputation, financial resources, ability to obstruct or cooperate in a venture, possession of something the other side desires, and so on).

At the opposite end are the assets held by the other side. It is a rare negotiation in which the scale starts out perfectly balanced (indeed, in most instances, one side has the clear advantage). Shrewd negotiators play their power chips much like a poker player. If you're at the disadvantage, you want to even the scales as much as possible (through astute bargains and shrewd bluffs); if you have the advantage, you want to maintain your advantage by keeping your aces in reserve.

One of your tasks during the preparation phase is to take an accurate inventory of the power assets in play, both your own and your opponent's. To help identify the power elements before starting the negotiation process, answer the following questions:

1. What is at stake in this negotiation? What are the specific demands? What are the underlying interests?

2. What is the net worth of my assets in this negotiation? What are the different chips I have at my disposal? What assets does the other side have?

3. In order for demands to be satisfied, what resources must change hands? Who controls them? What are they worth? (Remember, value is relative. To a starving person, a crust of bread is priceless; to a wealthy person, a full-course, five-star banquet is just another meal out.)

After conducting the audit, tally the power quotient by attaching numerical values to each asset in terms of its relative worth. Do this on a scale of 1 (limited impact) to 5 (very high impact). For example, assume you are negotiating to buy a business. The business is successful and in a desirable location. The owner, who is getting on in years, wants to retire and his children don't want to take over. He doesn't have the same amount of energy he used to and knows that much of the value of the business derives from his management. The business is in an industry that is currently prospering. He is highly motivated to sell while times are good. His power chips include:

- A prospering business with a solid balance sheet (+5).

- A good reputation with customers (+4).

- A vital industry at the top of its cycle (+4).

- Ability to act in a timely manner and authority to make the decision without consulting others (+3).

His exposures or power negatives include:

- He is getting older and wants to retire (–3).

- His children don't want the business so he has nobody to pass it on to (–3).

- He is eager to deal before the business cycle turns down (–2).

- Much of the good will with customers is related directly to him and may not pass along with the firm (–2).

His tally comes to +6

What's your situation? You want to go into business for yourself and are reasonably familiar with this industry, but not an expert. You have a sizable amount of investment capital and a strong line of credit. You would prefer not to have to displace your family, and this business is located near your home. You are in no hurry to make a deal, being in a strong position with the freedom to explore options. Propositions to buy other businesses are constantly being offered to you and because of your diversified background, you can go into a number of different industries.

Here are your power chips:

- Access to capital (+5).

- Time to consider alternatives (+4).

- Other business opportunities (+4).

Here are your power negatives:

- Reluctance to move your family (–4).

- Reasonable familiarity with industry but not expertise (–2).

Your tally comes to +7.

In this particular instance, you enjoy a slight advantage. What does this mean? Perhaps you can ask for additional assets to even the scales. Maybe the seller owns adjacent real estate that will make the business worth more. Perhaps he can finance the deal at rates below the bank. By calculating the power equation, you know in advance your strengths and weaknesses.

Any negotiation, from getting your kids to do the dishes to obtaining four tomatoes for a dollar instead of three, can be similarly analyzed in terms of power components. After finishing your inventory, you can establish who has the advantage and who has the disadvantage. This is critical knowledge. Even if you are at a disadvantage, it is better to adjust your strategy than to blunder foolishly.

TIME

The second element in the negotiation paradigm is time. As in life, it is the most elusive.

In negotiations time is relative. Situations alter, circumstances change, assets go up and down over time. A strong advantage today may become considerably less so a month from now; apparent weaknesses can change just as quickly.

In any negotiation, one side is usually more pressed for time than the other. They may be more in a hurry to consummate the deal—more desirous to make something happen quickly.

In preparing your paradigm, analyze the time component. What are the deadlines each of you faces? Is the resolution pressured by some deadline? Which assets are time-sensitive? Are you discounting/compounding future values? What costs do you incur if the deal is not done at the present time? What are the benefits to waiting? What are the lost opportunity costs?

A consideration of time tends to be less numerical than a calculus of power, but you can determine which side is more time pressured. When time is on your side, stalling and delaying are to your strategic advantage. When the clock is working against you, your objective is to identify those power assets that are least time-sensitive and extract maximum value for them during the negotiation.

INFORMATION

Information is the intelligence you gather to help you understand the context and thus play your cards to their maximum advantage—information related to your opponent, the goods/services for sale, and the general mood/atmosphere of the negotiation. (You would be absolutely stunned to know the number of people who enter into a negotiation without first accumulating adequate information.)

For starters, you need to know the value of what you're seeking. Don't accept the seller's evaluation; find out for yourself. Consult independent experts. Conduct research in the library. Determine what similar objects have traded for in comparable situations.

What do you know about the other side? Where do they come from? Who do they work for? If they represent a big organization, what is their position in it? Do they have quotas to fill? Why are they doing this deal? Are they negotiating from strength or are they desperate? Are they trustworthy (you'll find this out by talking to people who have done business with them before)?

 Knowledge Is Power   In the preparation phase, you want to learn absolutely all you can about the situation, the objects in question, and the consequences for the other side if they fail to make a deal.

The experience level of the other side is going to have an influence on the context. Have they ever conducted a comparable negotiation like this before?

When the other side is knowledgeable about negotiations, when they understand the interplay of demand and offer, you can negotiate with both greater freedom and greater watchfulness.

When they are inexperienced, however, you must tread more lightly lest they become spooked. They tend to take negotiation ploys personally (a low offer is considered an insult, a question of "Says who?" is a personal affront). They will also tend to rush the process, treating early round offers as fixed and final. They also tend to be less flexible and less likely to entertain creative propositions.

When the other side is less experienced, you have a slight advantage, but you should also watch out for certain risks. You cannot predict how amateurs will respond—they may take it as a sign of bad faith when you do not show the same sense of urgency that they feel, when you refuse to readily accept their bids.

tip **Be Humble** Always assume that you're dealing with seasoned professional negotiators who are sharper than you, especially when they appear to be playing dumb! If you really are dealing with amateurs, be cautious and diplomatic in your actions.

In this lesson you learned to evaluate the factors of power, time, and information that comprise the negotiation context.

REFINING YOUR INTENTIONS

In this lesson you learn to consider the intentions underlying your demands and how to be flexible enough to have alternative ways to achieve them.

As previously noted, a difference exists between demands and interests. A demand is a specific desire (a red Mercedes convertible, a room with an ocean view, a Saint Bernard puppy) whereas an interest is the underlying desire that gave rise to the demand (a spiffy sports car, lodging for the night, something warm and cuddly to love).

When a negotiation focuses on fixed demands, it risks hitting an impasse.

tip   **You Can Always Get What You Need**   In preparing to win, one of your objectives is to differentiate your demands from interests. Doing so enables you maximum flexibility in achieving your goals. Every negotiation has competitive elements. Don't risk losing the war because you insist on winning a specific demand at the risk of not accomplishing your interests.

What Do I Need, What Do I Want, What Can I Get?

Having options doesn't mean that you don't stick by your demands. Just the opposite! It means that you have skillfully developed acceptable possibilities, and therefore a range of acceptable options exists for you.

To be sure, there are always demands that are absolutely fundamental to achieving your goals. Except in extreme circumstances, however, you don't want to box yourself into a corner in which any single demand becomes non-negotiable. (It may be possible, when one party has a disproportionate amount of power or the other party lacks the will to resist, for a non-negotiable demand to be met. But a considerably higher price is paid for that kind of ultimatum, particularly if the two parties are destined to meet again another day.)

tip

Maintain Flexibility   Avoid putting yourself in a situation in which a single demand must absolutely be met. Even in extraordinary circumstances, in which you have a vital demand without which you will not accept a deal, don't announce that fact. Revealing such a demand to your opponent may harden the opposition and stiffen the cost.

In considering your demands, your goal is to find alternative ways to satisfy your essential interest. These alternatives must also fit a second requirement: They must be realistic.

Realistic Demand A demand that the other side can truly accept and that also increases the win-win content of the negotiation. Without weakening your own needs and demands, it considers the possibilities available to the other side.

For example, assume that you are preparing to negotiate with your supervisor. Your demand is a big raise in excess of company policy. What is the interest you are trying to fulfill?

You have more duties at home as your family grows; both you and your spouse are feeling the pressures mount. Both of you are working long hours, rushing back and forth to day care; your weekends are consumed with performing household chores and playing taxi; your marital relationship is stretched thin. Your true interest is easing the stress at home.

A raise may serve your interest, but that would require more than your boss can pay—it is an unrealistic demand. There are other solutions, however, that meet your criteria and are realistic. Being permitted to work flexible hours would help your situation. So would getting an extra week of personal vacation, being allowed to work from home a day or two, or even getting the company to start a day-care facility on-site.

Take another example. Assume that you are buying a new suit. It costs $500 and you want to negotiate to $400. Being savvy (and having read the earlier chapters in this book), you know that in every situation you are empowered to negotiate. Your interest in this case is to save money and increase the value of your purchase.

The store manager responds to your proposition, but is not in a position to cut the price (the suit is this season's inventory).

There are other ways for you to accomplish your goal. You can propose that the manager pick out a shirt and several ties that go well with the suit (thereby offering you more incentive to buy) and give them to you for free in lieu of reducing the price.

NEVER REVEAL WHAT YOU WON'T ACCEPT

When you establish your choices, it is important that each option is acceptable to you. Obviously, the last choice on your list doesn't look as desirable as the first, but the important point is that you are willing to live with it just the same. Why this insistence? Because your negotiation range needs to be credible in your own mind as well as to the opponent. Remember that any of these choices may end up as the final agreement.

You never want to reveal what you won't accept. Doing so limits your range of action. As soon as you blurt out that something is unacceptable ("All the money in the world couldn't get me to sell X!"), an option has been removed from the process. Perhaps all the money in the world plus that red Mercedes convertible might indeed have persuaded you to sell X but, because you already dismissed the notion of ever selling X, it has ceased to be a negotiation point.

KEEP YOUR EYE ON THE BALL

Distractions are a constant threat. They pull you away from your goal. They come in all kinds of sizes and shapes and tend to appear when least expected. Beware! They'll deflect you from your intentions and leave you wide open to being blindsided.

Hidden agendas are pernicious and can pollute win-win negotiation. Sometimes these hidden agendas are rational, but often they are subconscious, which makes them all the more difficult to manage. When both parties seem to be butting heads without relief, you may be arguing about issues not related to the negotiation.

For example, you may think you are negotiating with your business partner about office space—i.e., who will get the corner window in the new suite you've just leased—but you discover that you're really dealing with your frustration that he hasn't brought in much new business and his frustration because you are perpetually disorganized. A married couple presumes they are negotiating about how to decorate their apartment but she's actually angry that they are spending her big annual bonus on furniture when she wants to go to Acapulco, whereas he's had a lousy year and wishes he could have earned enough to pay for the Acapulco trip.

When the key issue lurks below the surface, you may need to re-frame the negotiation context in light of the ongoing problem. Be prepared to withdraw from the negotiation in order to do some self-analysis.

In this lesson you learned to consider the intentions underlying your demands and how to be flexible enough to have alternative ways to achieve them.

13

THE BUILDING BLOCKS OF INFORMATION

In this lesson you learn the importance of being prepared with information about the other side and how to acquire such information.

Knowledge is power. During a negotiation, what you don't know most definitely can hurt you.

A good general would never go into battle without knowing all about the enemy: the nature of its leadership, the size of its army, what kind of weapons and supplies it has, and the state of its morale.

A general would also want to know everything possible about the field of battle: Is the terrain flat or hilly, densely wooded or barren, sandy desert or tropical jungle?

Why is information vital? When you enter into a negotiation without adequate knowledge, you run two very real risks:

- First, you are setting yourself up for failure, because, in your ignorance, the other side is well positioned to surprise you. You are in danger of being blind-sided, having your plan undermined as you stumble unsuspectingly into a trap for which you were unprepared. You may end up scrambling just to keep up.

Avoid the Sand Traps What you don't want to do in a negotiation is find yourself in a hole in which you are forced constantly to improvise.

- Second, even you are not privy to opportunities and advantages that you might have easily grasped if you had done your research. You do your cause a disservice by being uninformed. You cannot, as the old saying goes, ask for what you do not know exists. In other words, the streets may be lined in gold, but if you don't know enough to look down, what good are they to you?

Information gathering is not difficult. Playing reporter can even be fun. Think of it as a grown-up game of "I Spy." Even so, lots of folks are intimidated by the process. They don't like to ask direct questions; they want to avoid seeming nosy. That's a fine approach at a church social, but not in a negotiation.

The More You Know   Need to know is the operative order of the day. The more raw information you have at your disposal, the better armed you are.

CREATING A PROFILE OF THE OPPONENT

When police investigators face a tough case, they create a profile of the person they're trying to catch. They create this profile from characteristics of predictable types most likely to commit certain kinds of crimes.

The techniques of constructing a profile can help you gather relevant information.

You need to be able to answer the following questions:

- Why is the other party participating in this negotiation?

- What other ventures are they involved in?

- How much personal interest do they have in your deal?

- What makes them tick? What are their values and interests; what do they want to accomplish?

- Don't forget their personal lives. Single or married? Divorced? Children? From a big family or an only child? Interesting recent work on birth order suggests that a person's position in the family group is a strong predictor of attitude: First-borns tend to be conservative and follow the tried-and-true, whereas middle and younger children are more rebellious and open to experimentation.

- How about hobbies? What newspapers and magazines do they subscribe to? What are their favorite television shows? Do they read novels? Attend the theater? Cheer for their college football team?

What's the point of all these questions? To understand the other party in-depth. A mistake many inexperienced negotiators make is to think they already know the other side well enough, and assume that the other party is "just like me" and want the same things. This is a dangerous approach. Pretend they are exotic strangers from a distant culture whom you must study like an anthropologist.

You also need to know a lot about the system that the other side represents. In many instances, the other side is negotiating not as an individual but as part of a larger organization, and are therefore subject to constraints and requirements that come from the organization.

FINDING INFORMATION

How do you find out this information? The answer is simple: *Seek and ye shall find!*

Taking on a research state of mind helps. Most of what you'll need to know is readily accessible.

Start out with standard library reference materials: *Who's Who*; professional directories (particularly useful with lawyers); *Reader's Guide to Periodical Literature.* If you have access to on-line services, search for their name and organization on the World Wide Web or in an information database such as Lexis-Nexis. Have they ever written a book? If so, read it to learn how they think.

Don't Believe Everything You Read   One word of caution: as a former reporter with national publications, I urge you to treat anything you read with healthy skepticism. Just because information is in print doesn't make it true. What you see in the papers and magazines is a version of reality passed through several filters. Use it for background; don't take it as gospel. Reporters and editors normally don't lie, they (like all of us) just see the world through their own particular perspective.

When you need to know something, go to the source. As you talk to the other side in the earliest stages of your dialogue, even before you've settled into a formal negotiation, make inquiries. Find out about their personal situations. Where did they grow up? How long have they worked within their respective organizations? What do they all like to do on vacation?

Getting third-party comments about the other party is often quite helpful (but again, add a dash of skepticism to whatever you hear). Without lying, you can introduce yourself to a potential source as someone who is "entertaining a business relationship with the party."

Putting Information to Work

After you have compiled your dossier and have a full profile of the party and their organizations, what do you do with all this information?

First, distill the raw data into news you can use. As you go over your information, ask yourself how each piece can help you accomplish your interest. Some of the information will pertain directly to your demands or help you plan your tactics (for example, the other party loves baseball, so you set up a session at a game; the other party loves Italian food, you therefore schedule a session over pasta; the other party hates romantic movies, you see a romantic movie just before your session and begin by complaining how much you disliked it).

Draw careful conclusions. From your research, can you identify the other party's *negotiation personality* (attacker/defender, accommodator, avoider, stalemater)?

BENEATH SUBSTANCE: MANAGING PERSONALITY ISSUES

Digging out the information blocks gives you a leg up in clarifying personality issues. There will always be negotiations with parties that have a history of hard-line bargaining and a reputation for being intractable. Simply put, they aren't very nice people (at least in a negotiation). Forewarned is forearmed! By separating the relationship issues from the substantive issues, you are better insulated from wounded feelings. If you have found out that the other party is known to be short-tempered and impatient, be prepared to make quick, direct presentations that speak to specific points. If the other party likes to stall and is indecisive, be prepared to be extra patient and not give away demands because you fear the negotiation is blocked.

By being ready for them to fuss and feud, you won't get sucked into their game and distracted from your own objectives (remember how the tennis star John McEnroe used to like to get his opponents upset so they would lose concentration?). By knowing that they pretend to be gentle pushovers who win every point by seeming to be too passive to resist, you know not to back off your demands even if their strategy is making you feel bad.

"BUY SIDE" TIPS

Here are five important considerations when negotiating a purchase:

1. A commissioned salesperson will almost always have more incentive to make a deal than somebody who is on straight salary.

2. Always try to make your biggest purchases from a vendor who is not doing well. Such vendors have more incentive to make a deal.

3. Always try to make your biggest purchase from vendors who are not located in high-rent districts; they have more flexibility to negotiate price.

4. When you are negotiating with a service industry (such as building contractors), place a premium on the stability of the organization and the length of time in business.

5. Sellers dealing for themselves are likely to be more emotional about the negotiation and less objective about price than a third-party seller.

In this lesson you learned the importance of being prepared with information about the other side and how to acquire such information.

"PREPARING TO WIN" WORKSHEET: WHAT I WANT TO ACCOMPLISH

In this lesson you learn how to compile a preparation worksheet for your negotiation.

This worksheet should be used to prepare for any significant negotiation that you are contemplating or about to begin. You should allow yourself about one hour to fill it out completely.

DETERMINING YOUR INTENTION

Write down in ample detail what you want to accomplish. Be sure to include your general interests as well as specific demands. Summarize your objectives with a clear, succinct mission statement. List each of your goals.

For example, your mission statement might be "to acquire a house in good condition on a quiet street within walking distance of public transportation." Or maybe your intention is to "sell a parcel of land to a developer who will pay a premium for its long-term potential and be able to close the deal within the next 120 days." Or perhaps "to spend my vacation with my wife on a camping trip in the mountains instead of visiting her relatives as we do every year."

The more specifically you define what you want to accomplish, the clearer you will know the set of goals that is your aim.

My goal is to: _____

My specific demands are: _____

_____

My fundamental interests are: _____

_____

In order to accomplish these, I need to: _____

_____

I will need the support of these people: _____

_____

Before I begin, I must make certain of the following details and facts: _____

_____

Now define the entire program in compressed terms that encapsulate your preliminary preparation. These terms provide the framework for you in developing your strategy:

In this negotiation, I will _____

by persuading _____

to _____

because I will in turn agree to _____.

DETERMINING YOUR MOTIVATION

Why do you want to accomplish this goal? What are your reasons? Take the time to spell them out. Often we don't know ourselves as well as we think. In order to have a clearer grasp of your actions, list all the reasons you can think of for getting into this negotiation.

For example, if you are buying a home, is it because you need more space? Or you want to move up to a better neighborhood? Or your mate is unhappy with the current house? Do you have a new job with a distant commute? Or you feel a new house will improve your family situation?

Maybe you want to sell the land because you need cash? Or have you identified an attractive investment opportunity? Have you learned that taxes are going up? Or are you moving to another location and don't want to be an absentee landlord?

Identify as many of your motivations as possible at as many levels as possible. Some will be less important to you than others and will serve as trade bait during the negotiation.

I want to accomplish this goal for the following reasons:

_____

Other secondary reasons I want this are:

_____

Reasons why my family, friends, advisors, and other people whom I listen to think this is important to do:

_____

Second thoughts, reservations, and reasons why I should be cautious and perhaps not do this:

_____

DETERMINING YOUR FALL-BACK POSITIONS

Before you enter into a negotiation, it is important to be prepared for the process to break down and your goal not be accomplished. Don't confuse this outcome with failure.

One of the characteristics of a successful negotiator is knowing when to walk away from a situation—this, in itself, is a form of success. You need to be armed in advance in case you need to abort.

Why is it possible that my goals may not be accomplished? _____

If I don't accomplish my primary goal, what will this mean to me immediately?

_____

What will this mean to me in the long term?

_____

What will be the single most important consequence of this not happening?

_____

If this negotiation fails to succeed, here are the alternative ways I will be able to achieve my goals:

_____

Defining Your Limits

Be sure to include elements other than money that constitute part of the "price."

Buying

I am comfortable paying a price of: _____

The highest price I will pay is: _____

The lowest price I can reasonably hope to pay is: _____

My time frame for paying is: _____

I can pay this much in cash: _____

Selling

I can comfortably sell for: _____

The least I will sell for is: _____

The highest price I can reasonably expect is: _____

How quickly do I want to be paid in full? _____

What surplus will I charge for the other side to pay over extended time? _____

Time

I expect this negotiation to begin:_____

I am prepared to spend this much time involved in the process:_____

I expect a resolution by (date) _____

I will walk away from this negotiation and seek alternatives if there is not a resolution by _____

Deconstructing the Other Side

The other side's (OS's) name: _____

Organization OS works for:_____

Title:_____

Responsibilities: _____

What you know about OS's background:

Birthplace? _____

Family history?_____

Education?_____

Marital status?_____

Children?_____

Interests?_____

What are OS's specific demands?_____

Underlying interests? _____

Time restraints and pressure? _____

What is OS's personality style (attacker/avoider etc.)?

_____

If OS becomes stuck in a personality impasse, what will you do to unfreeze the situation? _____

_____

THE INSTANT SETTLEMENT

After having concluded the worksheet, prepare a one-page settlement statement. This statement is written as a working document, a rough draft for the actual agreement. Sometimes, when you least expect it, the context of a negotiation evolves so quickly that you find yourself in a position to settle much earlier than anticipated. If that moment comes, you want to be the one to produce the working draft.

In this lesson you learned how to compile a preparation worksheet for your negotiation.

LET THE GAMES BEGIN: THE RHYTHMS OF NEGOTIATION TEMPO

In this lesson you learn the strategy and tactics of opening a negotiation.

Now we're finally ready to get down to action! (I was serious when I said you should plan to spend as much time in preparation as in face-to-face presentation!)

The first thing to know is that there is a rhythm to a negotiation. The comparison I use is to a chess game with an opening, middle game, and an end game.

In Phase One, the opening, your objective is to get your pieces into play, to get clear sight lines for your options so that you can fire them when ready. The opening is *not about trading;* it is about deploying your assets. In negotiations in which you have a considerable power advantage, your strategy may be to attack; in those where you are at a disadvantage, your strategy is likely to solidify your position and wage a war of attrition.

Let's pretend this is the first time you have ever formally entered into a negotiation. Before now, it has been mostly improvisation, catch-as-catch-can. You are probably a bit nervous as you say to yourself "On your mark...get set" but just before you whisper "go," remember that you are well armed: You have your objectives well defined, you know your trading limits, and you have a sense of what to expect.

Overcome Stage Fright Don't be captive to any outmoded messages playing in your mind. Enjoy the sport and challenge and excitement of entering into negotiation. No matter what happens, you'll gain more than if you didn't negotiate.

In Phase One, there is much exploring by both sides. You are looking for signs of weakness and uncertainty in the other side. The other side will probe you the same way (so, like a good poker player, keep a calm look on your face and a steady tone in your voice).

Some negotiators try to get the other side off balance right from the start. They grab for every advantage—where to hold the meeting, who picks up the tab at lunch, what should be discussed when, and so on. Regard this as a strategy to provoke tension and hostility.

Know Your Objective Before each session, write down your specific goal for the meeting. Why are you and the other side getting together? What do you expect to come out of this session? By defining your intentions, you increase the probability of attaining them. You also give yourself an opportunity to measure progress.

For early Phase One meetings, your specific objectives should look something like this:

1. Communicate our basic interests while revealing as little as possible about specific details. (For example, you enter an automobile dealership and say you're interested in "a high-performance late model car" rather than "this year's four-door turbo-charged hatchback model in black.")

2. Test your assumptions about the other side's basic interests. ("I assume a car like that is in great demand and will sell for a premium and take forever to locate?")

3. Explore the other side's organizational position and personal style. Are they free to bargain or subject to strict approval? Patient or uptight? Willing to banter or eager to close? ("Does your boss ride roughshod over you, or can you and I make a deal ourselves?")

4. Establish the ground rules of the negotiation—deadlines, specific conditions.

MAKING THE FIRST OFFER

The concluding part of Phase One is when the first offers get made.

It is almost always to your advantage not to make the first offer. It's better to be a counter-puncher than lead with your chin. *It is always to your advantage not to mention money first.* When the other side knows how much you'll give or what you'll take, they start whittling away from there.

In your first offer, avoid areas that are likely to prove the most difficult stumbling blocks. For example, your teenage son wants a car and you have already decided to help him buy one. He wants a hot sports car, but you want him to drive a safe, stodgy sedan. You also will insist he get a part-time job and maintain good grades. In your opening offer, you might say "I'll help you buy a used 1980 Chevrolet Impala." (This is the bottom end of your negotiation range; you're prepared to accept a flashier car.)

tip   **Make Demands Carefully**   By making the first offer, you're indicating that the negotiation is ready to proceed into its next phase. Don't give away the whole ball of wax with your first offer. You don't have to present all your demands at once. Indeed, it is best to maintain a few demands in reserve for Phase Two. You should not make all your demands in the opening phase.

BAITING THE WATERS WITH CHUM

When you go deep-sea fishing, you bait the waters with *chum*—chunks of bait big enough to catch the interest of your prey and lead them to take the hook. The same rule applies in a negotiation. Make sure that you have bait in the form of secondary demands that exist solely for the sake of trading off against your prime demands.

In the preceding example, "chum demands" might include washing the family car twice a month (because before, he used to clean it only prior to going on a big date), picking up his little sister from soccer practice (so you won't have to be disturbed), dropping off the dry cleaning, and so on. These are not serious demands; you are using them to exercise more leverage over your principal demand, which is his getting a job.

RECOGNIZING A HIGHER AUTHORITY

As we have discussed, it is to your advantage to present a higher authority from whom you must seek approval in finalizing the negotiation. Even if there is nobody, you still want the other side to believe such a person exists. In the opening stage, at the same time as first bids get made, introduce into the dialogue the information that you will have to get external approval. In personal negotiations, you can suggest it is your spouse or significant other; in business negotiations, it could be your boss, financial adviser, lawyer, or business partner.

USING OPENING GAMBITS

In playing the game, make use of the following tactics whenever appropriate:

TACTIC #1: ALWAYS APPEAR RELUCTANT

How to present yourself: "I do not have to make this deal. I am interested in acting in good faith but I may or may not accept the conditions of this deal. That all depends on the terms. I have other buyers/sellers/options."

TACTIC #2: NEVER, NEVER, NEVER ACCEPT THE FIRST OFFER

How to present yourself: No matter how good the other side's first offer sounds, you don't want it! "Boy, that's attractive, I have to admit, but my concerns are still real." A good negotiator always starts you at one extreme of the bargaining range (highest for a seller, lowest for a buyer). No matter what they say (such as "This is a one-time only offer; take it or leave it!"), don't take it! If they really want to deal, they'll move from that spot; if they don't, you'll find somebody else who does.

Counter that first offer with what you think is an absolutely unrealistic counter-offer (far in excess of your own bargaining range).

TACTIC #3: "THAT'S NOT GOOD ENOUGH"

This is the single most effective way to begin the games on your own terms. Turn this response into an automatic habit and it will continually reward you. When the other side makes their opening offer, regardless of what it is, you simply say "That's not good enough," or "You're going to have to do much better than that." This knee-jerk reaction halts the other side in their tracks and makes them reconsider instantly (regardless of how they choose to react for public consumption). Be prepared for a seasoned negotiator to turn the tables on you and say "What will be good enough, then?" Don't bite. Avoid a direct answer.

TACTIC #4: CRINGE AND MAKE A FACE

A little bit of theatrical gesture goes a long way in a negotiation. At some point during the early stages, when the other party is presenting their position, shake your head in disbelief. Make a small sound of horror. Register shock and horror! Then stay silent (don't expound or provide an explanation).

This action delivers a strong subliminal message to the other side that they are dangerously close to violating your bargaining range and had best not stray too close again. Remember to keep your silence during this drama. This is not the time to make a serious counter-offer. This is the time for the other side to retreat in embarrassment and alter its offer.

TACTIC #5: ASK FOR THE KITCHEN SINK

Don't be shy in your first offer. That's a mistake professionals never, ever commit and amateurs almost always do. The more you ask for in the beginning, the better. Be bold. You're not being greedy, you're being aggressive. Eventually you will re-treat and strike an acceptable compromise, but not in the opening round. When you make excessive demands, you can always give things back that you don't absolutely require. If you begin by asking for A, B, and C and you'll settle for C, you can always trade A and B. But if you start out modestly with just C, what will you be able to trade?

TACTIC #6: NEUTRALIZE THE OTHER SIDE'S PERCEIVED POWER

The other side will try to make you feel slight and inferior in order to make you cower into submission. Let them try! Such things as one's profession, the organization one represents, or wealth as evidenced in wardrobe, car, jewelry, or residence all have very real influence in the status pecking order. But by recognizing this in advance, you can resist much of the power invested in the symbol. Your mission is to disregard these ele-ments and focus on your own agenda and strategy.

Tactic #7: Schedule Sessions on Your Own Turf

You are always better off with the home field advantage in the early sessions. (Later on, that isn't necessarily the case; you may want to exit abruptly for dramatic effect.) Negotiations, like basketball games, give an advantage to the home court. You control the surroundings. On your turf, you set the mood (whether formal or informal), provide the perks and privileges (ranging from whether to serve coffee or whiskey to when it's time to adjourn), and dominate the social rituals as host.

Tactic #8: Calm a Buyer, Agitate a Seller

If you have something to sell, you want the buyer to feel as comfortable, calm, and self-assured as possible. Provide refreshments and hospitality; make the surroundings attractive and restful. Avoid distractions. Answer every question and ease every uncertainty. If you have something to buy, follow just the opposite approach. Make the seller uncomfortable, jittery, uncertain of your intentions: ask too many questions; leave the session to take phone calls; drive across town to pick up your maiden aunt from the beauty parlor when the other side is itching to continue; consult your lawyer in mid-session.

Tactic #9: Use Confusion to Your Advantage

When people are unsettled, they are more easily influenced and persuaded than when they are sure of themselves and the situation. At critical moments, it is to your advantage to suggest a variety of complicated options. The more complex the package, the better. Mixed in with these options is the one that you favor, artfully concealed within the pack. Devote attention to those aspects of the situation that are hardest to understand; keep going off on tangents. Make distraction your ally. If you notice the other side using this tactic, don't become confused.

In this lesson you learned the strategy and tactics of opening a negotiation.

16

WINNING THE MIDDLE GAME

In this lesson you learn how to manage the middle stages of a negotiation.

The middle game is all about patiently controlling the process. Your pieces are in play. The other party has declared itself. In the opening phase, you defined your boundaries, established your presence, and demonstrated that you will not be bullied into submission. In the middle game, you dig in, display your stubbornness, and stake out your base to test the other party's stamina.

Now the two of you begin serious jockeying for field position.

Exchange begins in the middle game. Be careful not to get carried away. You are not yet into the main event in terms of trading (although the other party may try to lure you in). Some people compare negotiations to professional basketball: The only part of the game that really counts is the last five minutes of the final quarter. This is a slightly exaggerated view, but essentially correct. Patience is key at this stage!

 Save the Best for Last Eighty percent of the concessions in a negotiation occur in the final phase, often on the eve of a self-imposed deadline.

What does this mean to you? It means that you must pace yourself! Twice as much time is usually spent in the middle game as in the other two parts. This may surprise inexperienced negotiators, to whom the middle part may seem tedious. Don't be sucked in by the temptation to rush to a conclusion. Remember General Custer!

 The Goal of the Middle Game   You gain (or give away) most of your demands in the end game, primarily as the two-minute clock winds down. This means that you must use the middle stage to persuade the other party with your arguments and to convince them that your position is serious and firm. Don't expect any significant concessions, just keep hammering away at your main points. You also use the middle stage to test the convictions of the other party. (*Note*: If the other party does begin making substantive concessions, the negotiations may be accelerating into the final phase ahead of your time-table, so be ready to adjust.)

The act of keeping the dialogue moving is itself one of the purposes in the middle game. The more time and energy the other party has invested in the process of negotiation—meeting, writing memos, making telephone calls—the greater the incentive to reach an agreement. Keep them talking!

TACTICS OF THE MIDDLE PHASE

The flow of the middle game requires you to have a set of tactics that accomplishes two objectives:

- The first objective is to *keep the negotiations moving without giving anything away*. Don't think of this process as stalling. You are establishing and reasserting your position while you test the limits of the other party.

- The second objective is to *accumulate resources for the closing phase*. You should be winning small points (getting the other party fully invested in the negotiation, creating personal bonds, displaying good will, and so on) and carefully tucking these points away to play at the last moment.

The following tactics help you to make it through the middle phase coming out on top.

TACTIC #1: RESOLVE THE SMALL ISSUES FIRST

It is important to establish good faith at this phase of the negotiation. You are laying the foundation for the end phase, at which time you accomplish your mission.

With your strategy, you have determined your *primary* and *secondary* objectives. As the other party makes its position clear, try to differentiate between their primary and secondary goals.

Often during the early stages of the middle game, it seems impossible to resolve highly divergent positions. Indeed, you may believe the task is impossible. Don't fret. And don't get bogged down about those seeming impasses.

At this stage, attend to the secondary issues (no matter how trivial). What's the point? These resolutions, however small, show that you're looking for ways to solve problems—to keep the dialogue moving with momentum.

TACTIC #2: KEEP AN IMPASSE ALIVE WITH SET ASIDES

In nearly every negotiation, there is a moment during this middle phase when it appears that nothing can be resolved. Experienced negotiators expect this moment. Whereas amateurs may throw up their hands in frustration and assume all is hopeless, a professional negotiator practices the art of *set asides*.

Set Aside   An issue you agree to disagree on until a later date.

When faced with a disagreement that resists progress, don't beat yourself to death trying to resolve it (even when it is a primary issue). Agree with the other party to *set aside* the issue temporarily and proceed with another subject.

tip   **Set Aside Emotional Issues**   Let a hot potato cool before you try to pick it up.

TACTIC #3: AVOID THE EMOTIONAL LAND MINES

Don't wave any red capes in front of your charging bull. During this stage of the negotiation, intense emotional elements normally surface (ranging from ego wounds and imagined insults to tangible issues of trust and honesty).

TACTIC #4: DON'T OVER-REACT WHEN THE OTHER PARTY SAYS NO

Hearing "no" can be scary. The first time you hear it, there is a foreboding finality to it. But remember, seasoned negotiators understand that "no" doesn't mean "never." It is a position just like any other position, subject to changes and shifts.

 Where Is "No" Coming From?   When you hear "no," listen for the source of the objection. There are always reasons. Some are concrete, some emotional. Respond to the objective sources with substance; stay away from the emotional sources. Bury a "no" with more information without trying to persuade the other party to change their response.

TACTIC #5: BE CAREFUL OF THE TELEPHONE

The telephone is a double-edged sword. It speeds up the process of communication and greatly facilitates the initial stages of a negotiation. It can, however, bog down movement in the middle phase.

Why? Because the telephone is a one-dimensional communication tool. It transmits words (and to some degree the emotional content behind the words, although incompletely and sometimes inaccurately). It fails to transmit visual cues and body language. On a telephone, one receives only a portion of the message. In a negotiation, partial communication can leave both sides confused and ineffective.

The advantage of a telephone exchange belongs to the person making the call. The caller intrudes into the receiver's space and time, disrupts the receiver's actions, and forces the receiver to adjust to the caller's agenda.

A classic display of this "intimidation by intrusion" is when a call is placed by the caller's secretary, and the receiver, who has been interrupted, is forced to wait on the line until the caller is ready. For these reasons, avoid being the receiver whenever possible. A good tactic is to tell the caller you are currently detained, but you will call back shortly.

TACTIC #6: GET IT IN WRITING

At this stage in the process, it is critical that the foundations for future concessions be laid. In order to achieve optimum results, you want to start nudging the agreement toward eventual compromise. A good way to do this is to summarize each step in written form.

After each meeting or telephone conversation in which you come to an agreement, write a summary. This summary doesn't have to be elaborate or formal, just something simple:

> "... as per our session of (Date), we agreed to the following points. We disagreed about the following points."

 Maintain a Record of Agreements   Spoken agreements disappear as soon as they are spoken. Written agreements, on the other hand, are preserved in a permanent record.

These memos are not meant to be binding. Although preparing them is a bit of a nuisance and requires discipline, regard the act as another way to manage the process. By writing the memo, you control how the situation is being recorded and perceived. When the other party signs off on the memo, they are ratifying your vision (or redefining it with your participation, facilitating dialogue).

Later in the game, these memos help put the negotiation on solid footing. It is much harder for either side to retract a position when it is written down.

Avoiding Traps in the Middle Phase

The pitfalls of the table. Although typical negotiations are filled with images of the bargaining table, cooperative dialogue is better served by a more informal atmosphere. The physical table can serve as a symbol of opposition as the two sides face off across from each other. The bigger the table, the more people tend to sit around it, further complicating communication. Sessions held in more informal settings with fewer people generally result in more productive dialogue.

Strength in numbers. A heavy-handed but effective tactic of intimidation is to out-number the other party. You show up alone; the other party brings in the lawyer, the accountant, the executive vice-president, and so on.

A variation of this theme is the "good cop/bad cop" routine in which you're negotiating with more than one person. One person is aggressive and tough; the other is much more sympathetic to your point of view. Don't fall for it! They both have the same goal—to get you to back down.

Creating a safe atmosphere. Even in an adversarial negotiation, it is in your best interest that the dialogue be open and honest. You don't want to contaminate the communication process with unintended signals or hostile messages that put the other party on the defensive. Avoid cues that can be taken as confrontational. For example:

- Statements that emphasize "you" tend to be viewed as accusations. ("Why do you want to have dinner with the Joneses?" makes the other party obliged to justify themselves.) It is better to make "I" statements. ("I find the Joneses dull; can't we find something else to do?")

- Forceful hand gestures, finger pointing, and fist shaking are perceived as aggressive behaviors. (If you have a tendency to talk with your hands, try to keep them in your lap.)

- Moving into the other party's personal space is threatening. (Conduct dialogue at an appropriate social distance.)

- Defensive body language such as folded arms, crossed legs, and indirect eye contact acts to create social distance and makes the other party suspicious. (When presenting your position, uncross your arms and look directly in their eyes).

In this lesson you learned how to manage the middle stages of a negotiation.

17

THE END GAME: CLOSING THE DEAL AND WINNING THE NEGOTIATION

In this lesson you learn how to recognize the end phase and structure your exchange of demands.

This is the moment of truth! It is in this final phase, which usually lasts about a quarter of the entire negotiation time, that most issues are resolved. Not before. Be ready for surprises—and be ready to spring some of your own.

As was continually emphasized in this book, good negotiators look for an array of issues that influence decisions; the interrelated demands and interests that constitute the *system of the negotiation*. Less skilled negotiators may try to reduce the process down to one or two elements. In the end, the side with the best understanding of the factors and the most chips on the table has the best odds.

---

tip **Keep Your Silver Bullets in Play** The more of your demands still alive up to the end, the more likely you are to win what you want.

You want to come from as strong a position as possible. You want the other party heavily invested in the process. You also want the other party slightly off-kilter, 80 percent confident it can accomplish its principal objectives, but not entirely certain that you'll agree to a final deal.

SETTING DEADLINES

Step one of the end phase is announcing a deadline.

You want to be the one to suggest that the game is drawing to an end. It suggests your willingness to do the deal but also communicates that you are not prepared to spend forever in negotiation. It tells the other party that time is running out.

Don't make this announcement as an ultimatum. This is not your "drop dead" date.

Don't deliver the news in an emotional outburst, but rather as a rational, well-considered decision that is in the interests of both sides. Frame it like this:

> "If we can't get to an agreement in several weeks (fix the date), I suggest we put this negotiation on hold for an indefinite period and then perhaps pick it up again at some future time."

Make sure the date is far enough in the future to be reasonable but not so distant as to fail to create a sense of urgency.

tip

Countdown to Victory   The other party needs to hear the clock ticking. They need to understand that the time has come to deal earnestly and seriously.

Don't Be Totally Rigid   One warning: Don't be totally rigid. You don't want to be trapped by your own deadline (that could mean throwing the baby out with the bathwater). The other party may test your seriousness and perhaps push past your time limit. Indeed, you should expect this. As long as the negotiations are moving productively at that point and the end is in sight, allow one brief extension. If they stall too much, you're out of there!

Motivate the Other Side   Until you set a deadline, chances are good that the negotiation will never pass from discussion to action.

RECEIVING A DEADLINE FROM THE OTHER PARTY

The other party will be pursuing the same strategy in terms of closure. They'll want you off *your* stride. What do you do when you receive a deadline from the other party?

Be prepared. What if they say "We need a decision now!"? For starters, it may well be their intention to limit your options by manipulating your reaction time. Why are they in such a hurry? If they absolutely insist but you don't feel sufficiently confident about the terms, don't accept them.

Look Before You Leap   The law of lesser evils says that it's always better to miss out on a good deal than live with a bad one.

A PRIMER ON TRADING

Concessions are part of the game; they are part of the process from the get-go and *not* a sign of weakness! Stubborn and shrewd are not synonyms. That's why it is called *negotiation*. Although you make exchanges at different moments, the bulk of them come in the end. It is at this point when you want to be your sharpest.

1. Don't assume the other party knows what you want. Speak your demands loud and clear!

2. Give with one hand; take with the other. Whenever you make a concession, be sure to extract something in return. Don't be shy. You're not doing anybody favors by giving away something for nothing—the other party won't respect you and you hurt yourself. Make this an invariable principle in your negotiation. Never give up anything without getting something in return (even if the concessions are trivial or symbolic).

3. The tit-for-tat concession allows the two sides to exchange demands of similar value. You offer to buy the floor model of the computer in return for a 90-day free service guarantee. You let your neighbor borrow your lawnmower if she fills it with gasoline.

4. Trading up adds value to your side (much like chess when you exchange your white pawn for the black bishop). The other party wants something small but important; you counter with something big. The store wants to sell the floor model to clear its inventory; you agree in return for a reduction of 50 percent. Your neighbor always borrows your

lawnmower; you give it to her one more time provided she has it tuned up.

In this lesson you learned how to recognize the end phase and
structure your exchange of demands.

18

TACTICS OF THE END GAME

In this lesson you learn the tactics of closing the deal.

The bids are on the table. Asking prices are whittled down, and offers are wedged up. The bargaining in secondary demands looks like option trading on Wall Street. The clock ticks louder and louder as the curtain begins to fall. Nerves are frazzled, tempers over-caffeinated. Welcome to the wonderful world of the 11th hour of the end game.

PRINCIPLE #1: ALLOW THE OTHER SIDE TO MAKE THE FIRST OVERTURE

Even though you called for the deadline, you want the other side to play their cards first when it comes to revealing what they will accept.

PRINCIPLE #2: WHY NOT SPLIT THE DIFFERENCE?

As soon as someone suggests splitting the difference, the whole game changes. These are the magic words. Keep your ears peeled for them.

The side that makes the offer has essentially revealed what it will settle for. By doing that, they give the other side a very substantive tactical advantage.

Here's the reasoning. Suppose that after considerable bargaining, you as the buyer are offering $100,000 and the seller wants $150,000 for a waterfront condominium. The seller says those magic words, "Let's split the difference." What the seller has just done is shrink the top of his acceptable limit by $25,000 to $125,000. You know he will accept that! What you don't yet know is the bottom of his acceptable limit.

The negotiating range has changed. Before, the difference was $50,000. Now it is $25,000 ($125,000–$100,000) and still in flux.

What's your move? Acknowledge the offer with appropriate respect but make it clear that you cannot yet accept because the price is still too high. (Continue to maintain that the top of your limit is $100,000.) Shift the dialogue to other issues (partly for diversion, and partly to maintain his high level of discomfort, which will encourage him to trade away secondary demands). After waiting him out, it becomes your turn to offer to split the difference. But now the negotiating range is between $125,000 and $100,000. You say "Let's meet mid-way; I'll go up $12,500 and you come down $12,500."

The deal is struck at $112,500.

 tip

How 50/50 Equals 75/25   Split the difference and you get 50 percent of what's in the middle. Split the difference after *they* split the difference and you get 75 percent.

PRINCIPLE #3: LAY PLANKS THROUGH THE QUICKSAND

What can you do if you hit a serious impasse in the final phase? The other side digs in its heels and can't be budged. Neither can you. After all the work and time, your negotiation is in real danger of collapsing. What are your options besides giving in?

1. **Buy now, pay later.** This frees you both up to keep going by agreeing to a temporary solution. Accept in principle enough major demands on each side to provide the framework to the deal and then agree to have others on both sides (lawyers, assistants, friends and family, and so on) work out the details. The agreement isn't officially enacted until those details are finalized, but both sides can proceed in the interim as if they have an agreement and behave accordingly. That means you can start to work together, to "try out" the solution. As both sides begin to implement the partial deal, the original objections that looked like they would subvert the deal may seem less large.

2. **It's the chemistry, stupid!** Late in the game, you and the other side hit the wall. You can't stand each other! No way around it. You think the room is too cold, and she wants to open the windows! But the substance of the deal itself is pretty much in place. What can you do? Change the team. Bring in some new faces. Have somebody else dot the i's and cross the t's. Just because you opened the deal doesn't mean you have to be the one to close it. Share the glory!

3. **Avoid ultimatums; offer choices.** "Take it or leave it" is like a nuclear bomb. If the other side knows you have it, they show you high levels of respect. But once you drop it, the landscape is too contaminated to support life. When you hit the brick wall, avoid at all costs the temptation to use this ploy. Even if you force a deal, you've made an enemy for life and may never receive full compliance. What can you do? Keep looking for alternatives. Develop option after option without dipping below your acceptable limit. ("You refuse to pay $10,000, but how about $8,000 now and $3,000 next year? How about paying $7,500 and throwing in your five-year-old Mustang? $6,000 plus roses for all the assistants at my company on Valentine's Day plus a golfing week in Palm Springs?") Whatever works. The possibilities are limited only by your imagination. Keep looking for the magic variation. Sometimes the key is something so outrageous that the other side can only laugh and agree.

Principle #4: The Last-Minute Surprise

The last-minute surprise entails throwing in an unexpected demand (usually not so huge as to break the deal but big enough to hurt) at the final hour, just when the other side has wound down its defenses and assumes you have a deal. Sometimes the last-minute surprise actually gets sprung at the signing ceremony for the contracts.

Personally, I think this tactic is foul play. But it's an option that you need to know about. If you choose to use it, do so only if your opponent desperately needs to make the deal and will give away virtually anything at the end to prevent the process from breaking down. The ploy may afford you a significant opportunity but it will earn you lots of bad karma.

At the same time, always prepare yourself for this possibility. Have a response in mind.

PRINCIPLE #5: KNOW WHEN TO HOLD 'EM, KNOW WHEN TO FOLD 'EM

The end of the end game is when you have to make the ultimate choice: Are you in or are you out? Not all negotiations come to fruition. The happy ending is not necessarily an agreement. *Sometimes you win by not doing the deal!*

The power to walk out the door is absolute power. You never surrender it right up until the moment you shake hands.

If you reach a point in the end game when you are blocked and unable to accomplish your mission, where all other options have failed to ease the stalemate, be prepared to exercise your option to toss in your cards. An amateur poker player thinks you have to play every hand, but a pro knows when to call it quits.

 tip

No Shotgun Marriage   Be careful not to make the mistake of "over-attachment" to a negotiation. Don't be so wedded to the prospect of an agreement that you settle for less than your objectives. It's better to return another day and play in another game.

PRINCIPLE #6: YOU DRAFT THE DOCUMENT

When it comes time to write up the agreement, you want to be the one who supplies the words. There's always more than one way to decipher the definitions, explanations, and conclusions in a document (that's how lawyers earn their fees!). Better to start the final go-round with your interpretation and proceed from there. Don't try to write a masterwork for the ages or try to mimic legalese, just provide a good solid summary of the points of agreement. Be specific about things such as dates, figures, and responsibilities.

PRINCIPLE #7: IT AIN'T OVER UNTIL IT'S OVER

"Done deal!" You've achieved a solid agreement. Congratulations. But agreement is only part of the battle. The other part is having the terms honored the way each side says they will.

The chances of such compliance go up dramatically when the negotiation has been conducted in an atmosphere of respect with a win-win spirit. Make sure it's in the interest of the other side to honor the deal!

tip

Victory Defined   The greatest negotiator is not the one who scoops up every last chip left on the table but the one whose mission is fulfilled and who still leaves the other side wanting to come back another day to do another deal.

In this lesson you learned the tactics of closing the deal.

INDEX

O

P